FOREWORD

ALMOST TWO THOUSAND years ago, at the age of 62, the Roman Emperor Septimius Severus came to Britain and astonished everyone with his energy and vision. He restored the province to Roman government, campaigned against the northern barbarians, repaired Hadrian's Wall and ordered the rebuilding of the defences of the Roman fortress at Chester, which still form part of the red sandstone City Walls.

It is a matter of pride to everyone who lives and works within Chester that exactly the same spirit is evident in the preservation and enhancement of the City and its surrounding countryside. To successfully combine commerce, industry and tourism, while meeting the needs of the local community, is clearly an enormous challenge.

My own personal commitment to the community of Chester, together with that of my fellow executive directors at North West Securities, is strong. We are proud to be involved in many forms of sponsorship relating to this historic city and will continue to encourage its society and development.

As a finance house, North West Securities' roots in Chester reach back to 1949 and a modest office in Newgate Street. By the time the first Conservation Study had been commissioned by the City Council in 1966 we were settling into a large purpose built nerve centre close to the Italianate railway station. Today, North West Securities is a national organisation with assets of over £1 billion, still based firmly in Chester and employing more than 2,000 people.

This report holds a great deal of optimism for the future of Chester and its surrounding areas, and it will be a useful reference for conservation bodies facing similar problems in any part of the world.

The commitment of the team that has made possible the success recorded in this document is a lesson in integrity, reflected in the many awards they have already won. May we take this opportunity to wish them ongoing success.

C. H. Bush FCIS
Managing Director, North West Securities Ltd

HISTORIC ROAD SURFACE IN ABBEY SQUARE.

Donald W. Insall

OBE, FSA, RWA, FRIBA, FRTPI, SPDip (Hons)

Conservation Consultant

Cyril M. Morris

JP, B Arch, DipTP, RIBA

Director of Technical Services

THE EASTGATE CLOCK.

PREFACE

TWENTY YEARS AGO, the late Richard Crossman invited four local authorities to join in commissioning reports on the problems facing historic cities. 'Chester: A Study in Conservation' was published in 1968; and as a result, the City launched an ambitious Conservation Programme.

Ten years ago, Donald Insall and I undertook the first major review of this Programme. We concluded that in most respects the conservation picture in Chester had improved out of all recognition. However, significant problems remained; and we identified both individual buildings and areas which needed priority action. We recognised the value of periodic assessments and recommended that a further review should take place in 1986.

The scale of the problem faced by the City Council, and the success of the Conservation Programme, may be judged from this report. This success has been a team effort, not only by the technical advisers, but also by the Historic Buildings Council for England (succeeded in 1984 by the Historic Buildings and Monuments Commission for England), the City Council and the Citizens of Chester. My particular thanks are due to successive Chairmen of the Development and Planning Committee and to the former and present Chief Executives of the Council, all of whom have supported the need for continuity in the Programme and for adequate financial resources to be allocated to the Conservation Fund.

I also wish to acknowledge the work of the present Conservation Officer, Andrew Brown, who has been responsible for the research and drafting of the major part of this report.

This review sees the completion of Donald Insall's conservation consultancy, which has spanned twenty years from the preparation of the original report. His influence in guiding and advising on the Programme has been immeasurable. I know that his concern for the City and its architectural heritage will continue and it is my hope that it will be possible for him to maintain a link with the City in the future.

In our previous report in 1976, Donald Insall and I wrote: 'Conservation is not about living in the past; it is the creation of an environment within which our architectural heritage can survive for future generations.' Our recommendations in this report reflect this constant objective. Problem buildings and areas remain to be tackled; we and our successors must be constantly vigilant to maintain the high standards which have already been achieved.

C M Morris
Director of Technical Services

CONTENTS

Foreword 3

Preface 5

Contents 7

A: Introduction 11

B: The Past Twenty Years 15

C: Study Areas 33

D:Achievements, Failures and Problems 95

E: Future Context 113

F: The Continuing Programme 135

G: Appendices 147

Bibliography

In preparing this Review extensive use has been made of the following studies and reports. Abbreviated titles have generally been used throughout the text.

Greenwood, Charles *Chester: A Plan for Redevelopment.* 1945.

Grenfell Baines, G. *Chester: A Plan for the Central Area.* 1964.

Insall, Donald W. and Associates *Chester: A Study in Conservation.* 1968.

Chester City Council *Chester Conservation Review Study, Rural Areas.* 1976.

Chester City Council *Chester Conservation Review Study, Urban Areas.* 1976.

Insall, Donald W. and Department of Environment *Conservation in Action: Chester's Bridgegate.* 1982.

Land Use Consultants *Visitors in Chester: A Study of Management Issues — Report on Part One.* 1984 [sponsored by English Tourist Board and The Civic Trust.]

Responsibility for compilation
While every care has been taken with compilation, no responsibility is accepted by the City Council, its Officers or Consultants, for any error or omission either in fact or opinion.

SHOTWICK HALL

INTRODUCTION

The Chester of today has evolved from nearly 2,000 years of history.

It is a city of contrasts, eloquent of its development; of strength and success on one hand

and vulnerability and failure on the other.

The physical shape and characteristics of the Chester we see today are, equally,

a synthesis of the architectural styles and social patterns of many ages.

Donald W Insall,
Chester: A Study in Conservation,
1968

INTRODUCTION

CHESTER IS BOTH typical and unique among Britain's historic cities. Typical because it has experienced all the pressures and problems of change that have afflicted historic towns over the past forty or fifty years. Unique in its determination to conserve the character of the city; the kaleidoscope of buildings from every century, set within the red sandstone walls alongside the river Dee.

The Second World War and its aftermath had brought years of neglect and under-maintenance to many historic towns. The urban recovery of the 1950s and 1960s was marked by the belief that urban problems could be best solved with comprehensive redevelopment and large scale planning. As the effects of these decisions were seen, the movement to resist the bulldozers and to preserve the heritage of our towns began to gain ground. In Chester for example, the campaign to save the fifteenth century Blue Bell Inn from demolition for a road improvement, led directly to the formation of the Chester Civic Trust.

One of the main problems in the conservation of historic towns is deciding where the balance lies between 'preservation' and 'improvement'. This is rarely agreed and seldom static. A town cannot be frozen in time. Each 'today' is only the immediately tangible part of an historical continuity. Conservation must appreciate this and must understand the past in order to plan how it can adapt to the future.

A planning scheme for Chester should aim at preserving the inner area as far as possible in its existing form and character, making such improvements and adjustments as may be necessary within its present structure.

These were the words of Charles Greenwood, City Engineer and Surveyor,

in his 1945 plan for the redevelopment of Chester. Although the Conservation Programme did not get underway until 1970, Chester had long been aware of the value of its heritage. The refusal to allow the demolition of the 'Nine Houses' in 1957, and the purchase of these seventeenth century cottages for restoration, despite ten years of difficult negotiations, is typical of the Council's approach to the city's historic buildings.

The economic value of the city's heritage was recognised in the Grenfell Baines Plan, 1964, which commented;

Chester's face is her fortune, it is the character of the city: its Rows and the charm of its architecture and environment generally which draws the visitor and which chiefly accounts for its high figure of retail trade per head of population.

There was also public appreciation of the city's buildings and of the benefits of enhancing the central area. In 1964 local amenity groups initiated a comprehensive repainting scheme in Bridge Street, which was carried out with the co-operation of local traders. A similar scheme was implemented in Eastgate Street two years later.

The Civic Amenities Act of 1967 was the first legal recognition of the importance of groups of buildings and the spaces between them. Previously, conservation efforts had tended to concentrate on individual buildings of quality, but this Act established the idea of 'conservation areas' and required local planning authorities to pay special attention to the preservation and enhancement of their character. While the Act was in preparation, the Minister of Housing and Local Government decided to commission studies that would examine how conservation policies might be implemented.

Bath, Chester, Chichester and York agreed to commission these studies jointly with central government. The objectives were to propose solutions for specific local problems and to suggest general lessons that would be relevant to all our historic towns. Donald W Insall and Associates were appointed to produce the study on Chester and survey work was carried out during 1966-67. Their report, 'Chester: A Study in Conservation', was published in 1968.

As a direct result of this study, Chester City Council agreed to establish an active Conservation Programme. A special Conservation Rate was levied, the first Conservation Officer was appointed and Donald Insall was retained as Consultant. This programme has been vigorously maintained over the past seventeen years despite economic inflation and restrictions on local government spending. It has been supported by the increasing acceptance of conservation philosophies by both the general public and the planning and architectural professions.

In 1976 the Council published the first Conservation Review Study, both to report on progress and to make recommendations for the continuing Programme. Its conclusions seem as relevant today as they did then:

Change has been rapid over the past decade, and in the present economic climate predictions for the next decade are impossible. Chester's architectural heritage has resisted many disasters over the past two thousand years. To ensure that today's heritage has a future beyond the next decade, it will be necessary to pursue an ongoing, positive and vigorous conservation programme, fully utilising all the resources available.

Regular reappraisals of the Programme were recommended, including a decennial review to provide the opportunity for long term assessment of achievements and policies. It is therefore appropriate that a further major Review has been carried out during 1986.

This Study has been prepared by the City Council's Department of Technical Services and Donald W Insall and Associates. It reviews the achievements of the Conservation Programme and proposes policies and priorities for the next ten years. By showing how Chester has tackled the problems of conservation, it is hoped that the study will prove useful to other historic towns that face similar problems.

THE RESTORATION OF THE NINE HOUSES IN PARK STREET WON A MAJOR CONSERVATION AWARD IN 197

13

*FORMER DERELICT BUILDING
IN SHIPGATE STREET.*

B

THE PAST TWENTY YEARS

Chester's being gutted - that's the only word for it.

Its entrails are being pulled out, the things that make it live ... I mean people and the

houses they live in. Without them a city dies.

Here, in place of them, a transplant is taking place, not of another living order to give

the body new life, but instead the centre of Chester is being filled

with a stomach of concrete and tarmac.

Rev Gerald Barlow,
Chester Chronicle,
1968

They will rebuild the ancient ruins and restore the places long devastated;

they will renew the ruined cities that have been devastated

for generations.

Isaiah 61 v 4.

THE PAST TWENTY YEARS

IN THE LAST two decades, Chester has visibly awoken as a delight among cities. The survey files of 1967 make strange and depressing reading. This was a place whose unique walled centre was very largely in decline, with whole areas of expanding decay. Residential life was withdrawing to the suburbs, leaving a scatter of empty houses which seemed fit for nothing but offices. Buses and lorries fought their way along the central streets and through a choking hold-up at the Cross. In many of the central streets, the enviromental effect of traffic noise was so damaging that it was measured and plotted, although surely no one would see any cause for this today. Despite the dawning urban recovery of the late sixties and the city's latent assets, Chester was uncertain of its role and hindered in its self respect.

In Bridgegate and other areas there was only dejection and hopelessness. It was widely believed that most of the buildings were 'past hope' and could only be demolished and redeveloped. Residents saw little future for their houses. One still vividly recalls meeting owners who had bought a new bath, wallpaper and pots of paint, yet relegated them unused to a cupboard, for fear of the future. Gaps and clearance sites yawned, warning notices proclaimed buildings as unsafe and environmental standards were desperately low. Key corner buildings like 'The Falcon' were empty and neglected, as the cost of repairs was higher than the value of the property. Double-decker buses, their engines running, waiting in groups in Lower Bridge Street, where nobody minded the fumes. The potentially superb riverside strand was thronged with people at weekends, but during the week it became a rat-run route of dangerous traffic avoiding the jam at the Cross. Corrugated-iron boathouses rusted between riverside houses and property values were

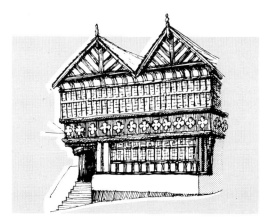

AFTER YEARS OF DERELICTION, 'THE FALCON' IN LOWER BRIDGE STREET WAS RESTORED IN 1979-82 AND CONVERTED INTO A PUBLIC HOUSE.

at their nadir.

Happily there were signs of renewing life. Commercial interests were beginning to respond to the possibility of precinct development; and the City Council had bravely taken up the traffic challenge by planning and driving through an inner relief road, to be aided by the future completion of the outer ring road. Architectural competitions were being held to infill a gap in unprofitable Watergate Street and for the redevelopment of the Market Hall site. The atmosphere was one of growing change and improvement; and there were positive hopes to be encouraged.

Donald W Insall and Associates accepted the commission to produce their conservation study of Chester in 1966. This examined the context of the city and its neighbouring towns, linked within a regional transport network. It noted the commercial trends and pressures; and, recognising that the city's prosperity depended upon its ability to attract the custom of the region, stressed the importance of making the best use of the outstanding, but latent, environmental advantages. Then it concentrated on the walled centre, studying the implications of a possible conservation policy; preserving, promoting and enhancing the architectural and historic quality of the area, with the aim of maintaining its life and economic buoyancy.

The most important asset of any place is its identity - the qualities which distinguish it from others, giving it character, individuality and integrity. The study recognised this and began painstakingly to appraise the townscape merits, the architectural quality of buildings, their ownership, use and condition. Over four hundred buildings were inspected in detail, outside and in, from attic to cellar. As a result of these inspections it became clear that there were major problems with the condition of the city's historic buildings:

A look behind the face of Chester's buildings reveals a widespread state of inner crisis, extending even to the heart of the City, the Rows. Defects in Chester's old buildings are fundamental, widespread and accelerating. In many cases they have reached a crucial state. The majority approach it, and some are sadly beyond it. If present conditions are allowed to continue, Chester's future status as one of Britain's foremost historic cities, must soon be in jeopardy.

The basic problem was the disuse, underuse and misuse of buildings. A tenth of the buildings surveyed were unusable because of their state of neglect, and many more were deteriorating rapidly towards that condition. This blight was spreading, affecting whole streets and areas, downgrading the environment and discouraging any improvements or investment. To ensure reality, range-figures for repair costs were provided for every building inspected and then grouped into a phased and practical programme of restoration and improvement.

The report emphasised the need for confidence in the economic future of the city if it was to attract the necessary investment for both the restoration of historic buildings and new developments. It stressed the need for a specific policy in a defined conservation area; and recommended a phased programme, including environmental improvements, pilot redevelopment schemes, 'first-aid' action, repairs and conversions. This programme identified 28 buildings in need of first-aid action that would win time for more comprehensive repairs, 142 in need of repair within five years and a further 229 requiring action as a later phase.

The full report was published in 1968, and was warmly welcomed by the Council and by local amenity groups. In January 1969 the Chester City Conservation Area was designated. Rather than identify only those areas of the highest quality, the Council took the bold step of including the whole of the commercial centre of the city within the conservation area, amounting to some 80 hectares and including 140 listed buildings. This included areas where substantial new developments were planned and was significantly larger than the area proposed in the report.

The Conservation Programme was established by the Council's Improvement Committee in December 1969 when it accepted the City Engineer and Surveyor's recommendations that:-

1   A sum equal to the product of a 2d rate be included in the estimates as the first step in the setting up of a Conservation Fund.

2   The opportunities for assistance available to owners of property in Chester be advertised extensively to encourage owners to take advantage of the existing grants and loans.

3   Letters be sent to the owners of historic buildings in urgent need of repair, detailing the financial help available and requesting their intentions as to the future of the building.

4   The Council enlist the co-operation of the owners of the buildings in Lower Bridge Street in urgent need of repair, to secure a holding operation whilst Government assistance is sought for a comprehensive solution to the problems of this area; and if the required co-operation is not forthcoming, the Corporation give urgent consideration to carrying out the necessary repairs to the unoccupied listed buildings.

5   King Street be approved for discussion with the Ministry with a view to a pilot project being devised to secure a continuing programme of repair and rehabilitation in the street.

6   Alternative traffic strategies be investigated with a view to establishing a traffic policy which would substantially reduce the number of vehicles in the city centre after the completion of the Inner Ring Road.

7   Consideration be given to the making of a direction under Article 4(1) of the Town and Country (General Development) Order 1963 in respect of the Conservation Area (the effect of which would be to require planning permission to be obtained for certain forms of development at present exempt from planning control).

8   A Tree Preservation Order and replanting strategy be gradually established throughout the Conservation Area.

One further crucial element was the appointment of an officer with specific responsibility for the Conservation Programme. This new post was to be the essential link between the various parties concerned with conservation, both inside and outside the Council. The level of the post was important, being senior enough to consult with the Council's Chief Officers and to speak with authority on Council policy, yet junior enough to be fully aware of the details of work on the ground. The first 'Conservation Officer' in the country took up his appointment in April 1971.

It needs to be remembered that this initiative was taken during a period of uncertainty for the city. Early in 1970 Donald Insall described Chester as '...an area of rapid change'. He went on to talk of the City's competitors:

... jostling with it for trade and indeed for citizens themselves. It is against this background that Chester must maintain her economic attractions.

There was a strong possibility that other towns would develop as major service centres, particularly for shopping, and that Chester would become a quiet backwater, with little regional significance and a contracting commercial centre.

It was in this climate of economic uncertainty and disruptive redevelopment that the Council adopted its Conservation Programme - a firm strategy with flexible tactics.

Pressures need not only to be identified, but must also be watched and then rapidly combated before they become damaging. Similarly, opportunities may suddenly become 'ripe' and must be taken at that time. If this can be achieved, positive conservation will begin and gain impetus, and once established, will generate its own encouragement within the whole area.

This quotation from the first Interim Report on the Bridgegate Action Area sums up the philosophy of the whole Programme, but the early years concentrated on three main elements; the restoration of key historic buildings [see C.1.0]; concerted action in the Bridgegate area [see C.5.0]; and the control of new development, encouraging an attitude of sympathetic design.

This third element, encouraging sympathetic design, was of crucial importance. It would have been easy to have concentrated on the repair of historic buildings and areas, while ignoring the damage that was being done to the character of the city by large redevelopments. Such schemes resulted in the vacuous townscape of Pepper Street and the demolition of the old Market Hall frontage, the most regretted loss in the city. This policy has not been a total success [see D.3.8] but the damaging effects of ill-considered designs have gradually been minimised.

In 1971 the Council reappointed Donald W Insall and Associates as conservation consultants, initially to make specific recommendations for the Bridgegate Action Area. It planned to concentrate energy and resources on a section of the city that had suffered economic decline and physical decay over a long period. A temporary office base was established in Lower Bridge Street, to act as a focal point for local people; and a survey of the area, together with detailed inspections of 77 buildings, was carried out within a six week period.

The first Interim Report on the Bridgegate was presented to the Council in December 1971. This indicated that the general trend was still a damaging decline, with 49 buildings in need of substantial repair and improvement. The report proved most significant for its recommendation that the City Council should acquire five groups of key buildings for restoration. This policy was adopted and has remained an element of the Conservation Programme ever since. The Council prefers to acquire by agreement, but regularly uses its powers under Sections 114 and 115 of the Town and Country Planning Act 1971 to indicate its willingness to act. In fact, although compulsory purchase proceedings have been initiated in a number of cases, the final acquisition has always been by agreement. A number of the case studies illustrate the Council's use of this policy of acquisition [see C.3.1, C.4.1 and C.11.3].

Thus the early 1970s were dominated by the acquisition and restoration of key properties in the Bridgegate. This policy was made possible by the financial support of the Department of the Environment, which recognised that the Chester Programme was a continuation of the 1968 Insall report, researching and developing the principles of urban conservation so as to establish a national example for other historic cities.

Other activity was also in progress. A new List of Buildings of Special Architectural or Historic Interest covering over 700 buildings was prepared by the Department of the Environment, being effective from January 1972. The Northgate Brewery was demolished and an archaeological excavation started prior to redevelopment [see C.3.0]. The opportunity of 'Operation Eyesore' was used to clean the Gates in the City Walls, the Town Hall and other buildings. Meanwhile the County Council were undertaking the extensive restoration of Shipgate House and the adjacent cottage [see C.5.2].

Inevitably there were crises, like the rapid closure of the consultants' Bridgegate office when the roof of the building caved in. Similarly the deterioration of Gamul House, one of the most interesting buildings in the Bridgegate area, reached a critical point in 1972 when the roof began to collapse. This stimulated the Council's purchase of the property and restoration started the fol-

GAMUL HOUSE, LOWER BRIDGE STREET, BEFORE RESTORATION.

THE RESTORED GAMUL HOUSE WHICH WON A EUROPEAN ARCHITECTURAL HERITAGE YEAR AWARD IN 1975.

lowing year. As a result of all this activity, building firms were fully stretched. Advertisements for tenders for the repair of Gamul House brought no response and a contract had to be negotiated.

During 1972 the Church of England reorganised its city parishes and the three churches within the Bridgegate were declared redundant. In the same year a United Nations Conference received a report on urban studies and interpretation. This led to parallel developments - the formation of a Council for Urban Studies Centres and the idea of Architectural Interpretation Centres. On a visit to Chester in February 1973, Lord Sandford, Joint Parliamentary Under Secretary at the Department of the Environment, suggested that the Church of St Mary-on-the-Hill become an Urban Studies Centre and St Michael's be purchased by the City Council as a Heritage Centre. These proposals were

---

THE REDUNDANT ST MICHAEL'S CHURCH WHICH OPENED AS THE CHESTER HERITAGE CENTRE IN 1975.

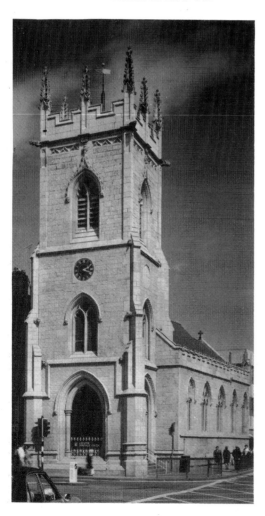

adopted [see D.1.4] and work began on the restoration and conversion of both buildings. The City Council also purchased the third church, St Olave's, for community use.

One of the major problems at this time was the increasing level of traffic, with its damaging effect on the attractiveness of the city. In the early 1960s eight trunk roads converged at the Cross, causing noise, smell, vibration, and hazardous confrontations between vehicles and the pedestrians who were confined to narrow pavements. Meanwhile people's attitudes to shopping were changing. Other cities and the adjacent new towns were able to develop traffic-free shopping centres with plenty of adjacent car parking. The completion of the Grosvenor Precinct in 1965, followed by the Forum, was a beginning; but as Chester wanted to retain its architectural heritage, the opportunities for redevelopment were limited. Alternatives had to be found.

The completion of the Inner Ring Road in January 1972 enabled the first steps to be taken to reduce traffic in the central areas. In March of that year the Cross, the very heart of the city and its traffic system, was closed to all vehicles except buses and the emergency services. This brought a substantial improvement; but it was a long way from creating a centre where pedestrians could relax and enjoy the city.

As people adjusted to the change, the effects were assessed and goals established for the next stage. After extensive consultation this was implemented in 1973 with the closure of certain streets to through traffic; and further changes were introduced in 1981 [see D.1.7]. This process of incremental improvement ran in parallel with the Conservation Programme.

The four city conservation reports [Bath, Chester, Chichester and York] published in 1968, had demonstrated that lack of finance was a major impediment to coherent conservation schemes. A Town Scheme of Grants was established in Chester for 1970/71 with allocations of £10,000 from both the City Council and the Department of the Environment (see

Table One.) This provided grants to cover half the cost of eligible repairs to historic buildings. Initially only a number of key streets were included, but for 1972/73 the scheme was extended to cover the whole of the conservation area. This joint grant scheme has proved a very effective method of encouraging owners to repair their buildings. The scheme is still in operation although the grant percentages have been reduced [see E.3.1].

In May 1970 a new flexible conservation grant from central government for the enchancement of conservation areas was proposed. These Section 10 grants were first used in Chester during 1973/74 to assist with work in the conservation area, the costs of the Consultancy and the employment of the Conservation Officer. Since 1976/77 Chester has been one of a number of 'programme towns', receiving a special allocation of Section 10 finance

[see Table One]. This financial support from the Department of the Environment has been essential to the Conservation Programme, as in addition to the repair of buildings it has encouraged improvements and adaptations.

The whole impression of these early years is of enormous pressure and a 'hand to mouth' operation for finance. The value of the Council's close link with Donald Insall is also apparent. In addition to his expertise with problems on the ground, he acted as a contact with national and international bodies. Throughout the period there was close interest and support from the members and officials of the Historic Buildings Council for England, who advised the Secretary of State for the Environment on grants for historic buildings.

In June 1973 the Bridgegate Action Area was selected as a 'Pilot Project' for European Architectural Heritage Year,

TABLE ONE
FINANCE AVAILABLE FOR CONSERVATION IN CHESTER 1970/87

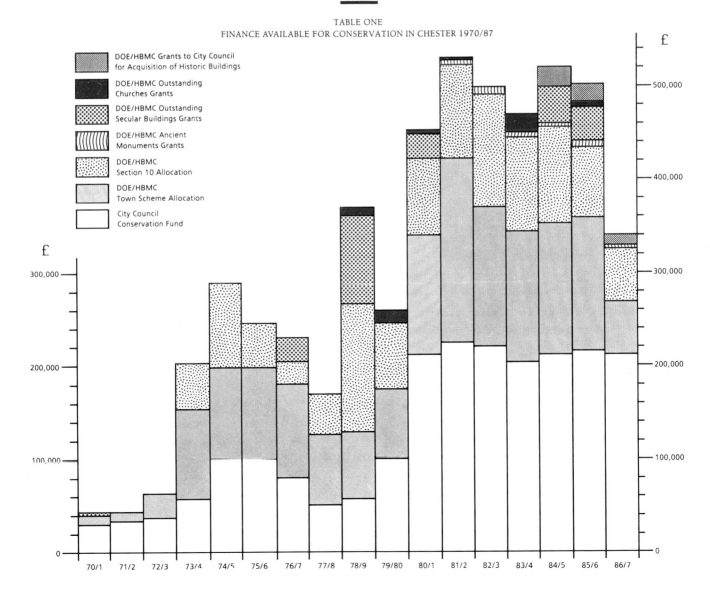

which was planned for 1975. This led to comparisons between the different national approaches to the problems of historic towns. It is worth quoting some of the thoughts that were expressed at that time:

Conservation in Britain is an integral part of land-use planning...a guiding influence upon the processes of change. In this way a historic town can be kept 'alive' and not frozen like a museum piece. The art-historian philosophy is most dangerous - you cannot 'put-back' a town to its original state - what is the 'original' in a living town? What one can do is to incorporate sympathetically into it, and then enjoy those earlier human strata which are so precious to it.

Letter from Donald Insall to the Department of the Environment.

Chester will be able and glad to show and to share something very British - not a national takeover, petrifying a town against its people, but a local and daily guidance of a living city through a Conservation Action Plan. Report by Donald Insall to EAHY Planning Meeting.

The preparations for Heritage Year began to absorb an increasing proportion

---

THE BEAR AND BILLET IN LOWER BRIDGE STREET, ONCE THE TOWN HOUSE OF THE EARLS OF SHREWSBURY AND NOW AN INN, WAS RESTORED IN THE MID 1970s.

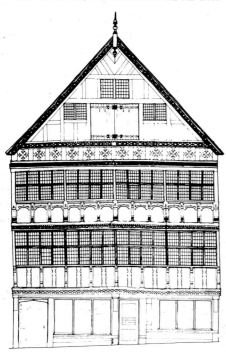

of the Conservation Team's time and energies. This coincided with a substantial build-up of work resulting from the seeds that had been sown during earlier years. In addition to work already planned, the first moves were made to secure the future of the Falcon and the Bear and Billet, two major timber framed buildings in Lower Bridge Street, and the second interim report on the Bridgegate Action Area was produced. In May of that year a Conservation Assistant was appointed, specifically to help with the supervision of grant aided restoration works.

Local Government Reorganisation in April 1974 could have created a major 'hiccup', but continuity of policy, councillors, consultant and staff was achieved. The Conservation Programme was strengthened by the appoinment of an architect as Director of Technical Services and the addition of another Conservation Assistant. Reorganisation also brought extra responsibilities; the new District covering an extensive rural area and including sixteen village conservation areas.

The new Council were concerned about arrangements for the locally determined capital allocations and a number of major restoration schemes had to be deferred. The problem was raised with the Department of the Environment, particularly stressing the fact that the Council were having to raise 75% of the restoration costs for their own buildings. This was particularly serious because almost half of the available funds were being used for buildings which the Council had purchased for restoration. Fortunately the Department agreed to raise their grants to 50% for Council owned buildings. Despite these financial difficulties the Conservation Fund allocation, a revenue item, was substantially increased.

Notwithstanding the concern over Chester's economic prosperity, expressed in the late 1960s, it became apparent by 1973 that the city centre was under substantial pressure to accommodate new commercial developments. A joint study by the City and County Councils was instituted; an interim report being submitted in April 1974. This indicated that Chester had experienced a significantly higher than average growth in office employment, with the completion of over 250,000 square feet of speculative office development in the preceding five years. Other major developments were being considered, [see C.9.0]. The report calculated that unrestrained demand could result in a further 500,000 square feet of shopping and 1,500,000 square feet of offices being constructed by 1986. This posed serious implications for the capacity of the road system and the historic character of the city. Both Councils, therefore, agreed to restrict new office development; allowing time for the preparation of long term policies in the County Structure Plan and the Greater Chester Local Plan. Applications for over 250,000 square feet of offices were refused over the following three years.

The Council were also determined to increase the number of people living in the city centre. This was a two-pronged policy; maintaining and improving existing housing in areas such as Gamul Place and King Street, and encouraging the provision of new units by conversion or by developments like the St Mary's Hill housing scheme.

European Architectural Heritage Year 1975, proved to be a very busy time for the Conservation Team, with Chester's approach to the problems of urban conservation provoking much national and international attention. The highlight of the year was the opening of the Heritage Centre in St Michael's Church by His Royal Highness The Duke of Gloucester. The Chester Civic Trust reinstated the partly fourteenth century High Cross to its traditional location outside St Peter's Church and the new Cathedral Bell Tower was officially opened. During the year a whole series of activities was organised; civic awards, heritage walks, repainting schemes, lectures, exhibitions, tours and study days. The city was full of international visitors and Chester's links with Europe, through Europa Nostra, were greatly strengthened.

As part of the preparations for Heritage Year, assistance was given with the Department of the Environment film 'The Conservation Game', which was to

have a very wide circulation. The year also saw the publication of a comprehensive report on the condition of the City Walls [see C.7.0] and the first editions of 'Conservation News', designed as a regular leaflet providing information on the progress of the Conservation Programme.

Early in 1976 the Council served Building Preservation Notices, under Section 58 of the Town and Country Planning Act 1971, on five nineteenth century estate cottages in Harthill. This was intended to prevent alterations which would seriously damage their historic character. The houses were subsequently listed and the Council have since made occasional use of this power to prevent similar damage to other buildings.

As part of the preparations for the 1976 Review Studies, which were jointly financed by the Council and the Department of the Environment, a detailed survey of the problems of conservation in the rural area was started. This Rural Area Study was presented to the Council in June 1976. Its main concern is still relevant today:

Under present policies, national aid is available financially only towards 'outstanding' historic buildings and 'outstanding' conservation areas. But the problems of many small villages in rural areas are equally intense and demanding and deserve careful attention in this context.

The two main recommendations of the study were that the Council's grant allocation for the rural area should be substantially increased and that a further twenty-one villages should be designated as conservation areas.

DERELICT BUILDING, ROWTON LANE, ROWTON.

From April 1974 a sum of £5,000 had been allocated each year for the rural area, but grants were restricted to repairs that were necessary to maintain the integrity of listed buildings and were normally only 12½% of the eligible costs. The study demonstrated that, even with these restrictions, the allocation was grossly inadequate to tackle the scale of the problem. Forty buildings were identified as requiring urgent repairs. Also the disuse and dereliction of agricultural cottages and buildings, resulting from changing agricultural methods, was recognised.

The Urban Areas Review Study was presented to the Council in November 1976. Following a survey of the condition of the historic buildings in the city centre, priority groups were identified to highlight the relative urgency for action and to take account of the resources available. Sixteen buildings or groups of buildings were given first priority status, indicating that repairs were necessary within three years. Ninety-six buildings were included in the second priority group because they were known not to have had significant work carried out in the previous ten years, despite having been identified in the 1968 Insall Report as requiring repair. An additional group of third priority buildings were recommended for further inspection. It was estimated that the next three years of the Programme could require a financial commitment of £500,000 per annum from all sources; a sum substantially in excess of the previously available funds.

The study drew attention to the importance of regular surveys to identify the condition of historic buildings and to provide an 'early warning system' on developing problems. This information allows the Council to take preventative measures, such as 'first-aid' repairs or warning the owner of potential legal action.

As a result of the emerging success of the Bridgegate Action Area, the study recommended two further Action Areas; the Cathedral Precinct [see C.2.0] and Queen Street/Canalside [see C.9.0]. It also recommended a number of other areas for ongoing study. Here the problems were often not 'pure' conservation and required

the development of other planning policies; traffic management, encouraging residential use or producing guidance for potential redevelopment opportunities.

Although the Council adopted the policies of the two Review Studies, financial constraints were to restrict the Programme for the next three years. The 1976/77 budget had cut the Conservation Fund allocation to £80,000, and further government strictures resulted in a drop to £50,000 the following year. The effect of these restrictions was partially offset by increased financial support from the Department of the Environment, particularly by increasing the allocation for Section 10 grants [see Table One]. Even so, priority could only be given to the most urgent repairs or to schemes that were already well advanced. This led to immediate concern that the deterioration of many buildings would continue, to a point where the Council would have little alternative but to condone demolition. There were particular problems in the rural area, as the publication of the Rural Areas Review Study, together with a series of public meetings about the designation of conservation areas, encouraged a steady increase in the number of grant applications. The damage done by the Council's inability to match this expectation with resources took many years to overcome.

Following the publication of the Review Studies and changes in the Conservation Section, the Conservation Programme Progress Meetings were reorganised. Previously these meetings had been primarily concerned with the Bridgegate Area and had involved virtually every department of the Council. This had proved invaluable while new ground was being broken; but with the Programme well established it was decided to restrict the normal attendance to the Director of Technical Services, the Consultants, representatives of the Department of the Environment and appropriate members of the Conservation Section. These meetings are held every three or four months and have been an excellent way of keeping track of all aspects of the work.

As a result of European Architectural

Heritage Year the Conservation Programme was well-known, and many people were wanting to find out what the Council was doing. In August 1977, one of the Conservation Assistants noted that the increasing numbers of guided tours were becoming a nuisance to all; interfering with the main work of the Team.

The County Structure Plan was submitted for approval in May 1977. This recognised the historic value of the city centre and noted its serious traffic congestion; establishing policies to achieve a balance between the quality of the environment and the need to maintain the city's position as a regional centre. It also established new policies for the rural area, abandoning the 'key villages' policy, which had seriously damaged the character of some settlements by surrounding them with substantial 'suburban' estates. This had been of particular concern in the Rural Areas Review Study. The new policies were intended to conserve the character of Cheshire's countryside and villages, while catering for the needs of the rural population.

In 1978 a report on the problem of vacant and underused upper floors in historic towns was published by the York Institute of Advanced Architectural Studies. This demonstrated that the future of historic towns and the use of upper floors cannot be separated. Chester was already aware that, despite its achievements, it was faced with a more deep-rooted problem than the building decay which results from age and weather.

Between 1978 and 1980 the City Council worked with the Manchester Polytechnic Institute of Advanced Studies on a study of the problems of vacancy and underuse in the city. It was clear that vacancy in peripheral areas occurred in isolated pockets and related to whole buildings being empty. Upper floor problems were concentrated in the commercial core, which consists of four and five storey Rows buildings with narrow frontages and little or no access at the rear.

A pilot study revealed that disuse was related to rear buildings as much as to upper floors [see C.1.0]. This led to an appreciation of the need to look at a whole block of buildings, rather than just at the upper floors on the frontages. Studying old maps showed that in the past, these areas had been penetrated with a network of small alleys and courtyards providing separate access to the rear buildings. Thus the concept of establishing new pedestrian routes through these landlocked areas was established; encouraging the use of rear buildings and providing new staircases to allow separate access to the upper floors. As a result of this study, an exhibition and audio-visual presentation, 'Chester - Stop the Rot', was mounted in the Heritage Centre during 1980 and linked to a seminar on the underuse of upper floors.

———

THE FIRST EDITION ORDNANCE SURVEY MAP OF 1875 SHOWS THE NARROW ALLEYS AND COURTS WHICH ONCE GAVE ACCESS TO THE REAR OF BUILDINGS IN THE PRINCIPAL STREETS.

A series of public meetings to discover the attitudes and expectations of the residents of existing rural conservation areas was held during 1978. Although most discussion related to local issues, a number of common concerns emerged. There was a strong feeling that conservation policies and grant aid for building repairs were meaningless while heavy traffic continued to damage and disrupt the villages. The need for environmental improvements, particularly the removal of overhead wires was stressed, together with criticism of a perceived imbalance in the Council's concern for conservation between the city centre and the villages. These concerns stimulated some increased activity in the rural area; but it has not proved possible to make much progress with the fundamental problem of heavy traffic and environmental improvements have been restricted by a shortage of finance.

In 1979, Chester commemorated its 1,900th Anniversary, and this included a Civic Award Scheme for Conservation. At the end of this year of celebration, editorials in the local newspapers indicated that the time had come to tackle the city's pressing problems. Despite the substantial increase in the Conservation Fund for 1979/80 and the signs of improvement in the Bridgegate, the general comment was that some of the momentum of European Architectural Heritage Year had been lost.

These comments are surprising when compared with the minutes of the Council's Development and Planning Committee for 1979/80. During that year fifty-five historic building grants were approved, sixteen conservation areas designated and a further four considered, a policy for the conversion of farm buildings adopted, the service of five Urgent Works Notices and two Repairs Notices approved and substantial repairs to the City Walls, St John's Church Ruins and the Rows steps implemented. In addition, twelve major historic buildings were reported as being at risk and a variety of appropriate actions approved, three enhancement schemes were initiated, the purchase of a stone mason's yard was considered and the remit of the Conservation Area Advisory Committee was extended to include the suburban conservation areas. An Article 4 Direction was considered for Tarvin. This would have extended planning control over minor house alterations; and although the idea was not pursued, the discussion provided the basis for later decisions to apply for such control in Albion Street [see C.6.0] and The Groves [see C.8.0].

By the beginning of 1980, restoration was complete or in progress on eleven of

LOCATION OF CONSERVATION AREAS WITHIN CHESTER DISTRICT.

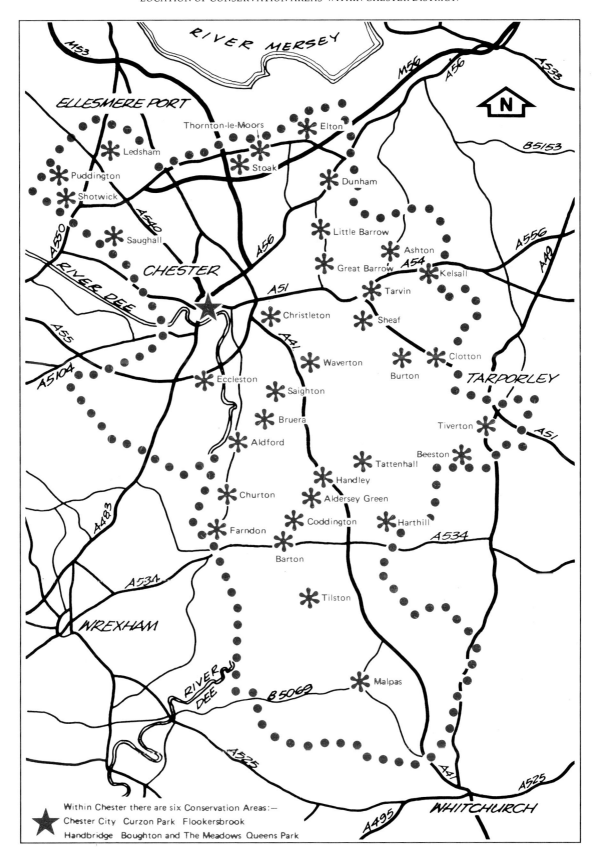

the sixteen first priority buildings identified in the 1976 Urban Areas Review
Study. Discussions were in progress on
the remaining five. Detailed surveys of all
the second priorities had been completed,
and as a result a further twelve first priority buildings were identified.

During consideration of the Council's
financial estimates for 1980/81, the Development and Planning Committee
requested a contribution of £199,450 to
the Conservation Fund, more than double
the previous year's contribution. The restrictions in finance over the previous four
years had made it impossible to promote
some repair schemes; the increase was
considered of vital importance to maintain
a satisfactory Programme that would prevent permanent and irreparable damage
to the city's heritage. In his budget state-
ment the Leader of the Council said, 'How
can we afford not to spend money to protect the investment in Chester's buildings?'. An increase slightly higher than the
Committee had requested was approved;
and the Council included this special
explanatory note in the rate demands for
the coming year:

*In line with the objective of maintaining
essential services the City Council has
increased the contribution to the
Conservation Fund for the next three years to
the equivalent of the product of a 1p rate
[£201,000 for 1980/81] in order to prevent
permanent and irreparable damage to the
buildings of the City's area. Although such
expenditure will not directly produce income
for the Council it is considered that by
improving and enchancing the value of
Chester greater investment from the private
sector and continued employment will be
encouraged. It will also help to ensure that
Chester remains as one of the country's
leading tourist centres and an architecturally
important city.*

These additional funds led to an
increase in the Town Scheme of grants,
with a new three year scheme being
approved by the Department of the Environment at £130,000 for the first two
years and £150,000 for 1982/83. The
Section 10 grant programme allocation
from the Department for 1980/81 was

£80,000. Some of these figures were later
increased again because of particular
pressures for grant aid. In 1981 the
Department invited the Council to undertake the full administration of the Town
Scheme. This delegation was agreed;
resulting in a reduction in the administrative procedures and a consequent speed-
ing up of the decision making process.

The early 1980s saw an increasing
involvement in work to enchance the
spaces between buildings. The cobbled
surface of Abbey Square was repaired in
1981 [see C.2.0], the programme of pedestrian paving in the central streets was
initiated [see D.1.7] and other smaller
schemes started. Plans were prepared for
reinstating the forecourt railing to the
Bluecoat Hospital, but these were not
implemented until 1985, when the
Chester Civic Trust adopted the proposal
to commemorate their 25th Anniversary.
During 1981 the City Council sought the
support of the County Council, as the
highway authority, for a policy to maintain traditional carriageway materials,
such as setts, cobbles, flags and wheelers,
and to reinstate these materials in minor
streets where they had been removed or
covered with tarmac. This was an extension of the policy on maintaining historic
materials for footways, which had been
agreed between the two Councils in 1977.
Despite the co-operation of the County
little progress has yet been achieved,
except in King Street [see C.2.0], because
of a shortage of finance.

The Council were delighted to
receive the 1981 European Prize for the
Preservation of Historic Monuments; the
citation reading:

*This award is intended as a tribute to
the exceptional services which the City
Council of Chester has rendered in preserving
the traditional appearance of their historic
town, in fostering its architectural heritage
and in adapting it to the requirements of our
age. In this work the Council has been helped
by the personal commitment of its staff and
advisers and by the judicious encouragement
of its citizens.*

*Here, after careful preparation and long
term planning and with the co-operation and
understanding of a public whose interest has*

been aroused, a work has been accomplished which, both in method and results achieved, is exemplary and merits recognition all over Europe.

The Prize money, given by the FVS Foundation of Hamburg, was used to produce an audio visual presentation of the work of the Conservation Team and to create a display of architectural masonry in the Town Hall Square, as a permanent record of the award.

This latter item was incorporated into a new pedestrian area, created as a result of the relocation of the bus exchange. The Town Hall Square had been clogged with buses for years; and the idea of moving them to a site behind the buildings to the west was first suggested in the 1964 Grenfell Baines Plan. By 1978 detailed proposals had been finalised; including the construction of a bus exchange, a new library behind the terracotta facade of the former Westminster Coach and Motor Car Works, and the creation of a pedestrian area where the buses used to stand. A large scale archaeological excavation was undertaken, generating considerable public interest and uncovering substantial evidence of the development of the city from Roman times. The whole scheme was completed in 1984, and brought a substantial improvement to the life of the city.

This period also saw renewed activity on the Council's own historic buildings. In 1979 the Director of Technical Services had reported that he did not have the staff resources to undertake a full programme of repairs and consultant architects were appointed to report on eight properties. As a result of these reports, three of the buildings were repaired and the other five were sold, on condition that they were restored. With the exception of No 93 Watergate Street [see C.4.0], it was made clear that grants would not be available for these restorations. This was part of a shift in policy by both the Council and central government, recognising that the attitudes of the private sector were changing and that, in some cases, restoration was an economic propostion without grant aid.

The Council's work in the Bridgegate Area was recognised in 1983 with the award of a Europa Nostra Medal. In presenting the award, Sir Gordon Pirie said;

The secret of success, if it is a secret, is not only the dedication and expertise of the technical advisers, both public and private, but in the mutual understanding of the Council and public opinion in support of the City's Conservation Programme.

That year also saw the start of the resurvey of the rural area for a new List of Buildings of Special Architectural or Historic Interest. It was already clear that the main emphasis of the Conservation Programme was shifting away from the city centre, but the new List was to confirm that change. Inspections of the condition of all the buildings on the former List were completed in the following year, and these demonstrated the dilapidation and lack of maintenance that were placing so many historic rural buildings at risk. The Council's increasing concern for these problems led to a steady rise in the grants made available through the rural budget, from £26,925 in 1981/82 to £79,774 three years later.

LOWER CARDEN HALL, AN OUTSTANDING TIMBER FRAMED HOUSE IN THE RURAL AREA, WHICH WAS RESTORED DURING 1984.

The report on Part One of the Visitors in Chester Study was published in 1984. This study was sponsored by the English Tourist Board and the Civic Trust in response to concern that the growing pressures of visitor and tourist activity could damage the historic environment. It concluded that, '... if such a threat does exist, it lies a long way in the future'. Nevertheless action is required and a draft Visitor Management Strategy is being considered at present. This includes proposals for environmental improvement:

It is recommended that a separate programme for improvement of these areas should be established by the City Council and that funds should be made available on an annual basis for progressive implementation of the programme using the model of the architectural review which has been so successful within the City Walls.

The summer of 1984 was particularly heartening for the Conservation Team. The end of the Kings Buildings saga was in sight [see C.3.1], work on the site of Nos 34-42, Lower Bridge Street was well advanced [see C.5.0] and the future looked hopeful for all the remaining problem buildings in the Bridgegate Area. The imposing facade of the Pepper Street Methodist Chapel was uncovered after being hidden for 50 years; major repairs were in progress at Lower Carden Hall; and plans for the restoration of the Grosvenor Park Baptist Church [see G.9.1] and the West Wing of Chester Station [see G.10.1] were well advanced.

In the 1985 Awards for Planning Achievement, the Royal Town Planning Institute highly commended the efforts of both the City Council and Donald W Insall and Associates:

All individuals and bodies involved have shown remarkable perseverance in a sustained and well executed series of projects to conserve the city centre while encouraging new developments of high quality, sensitive to the historic environment.

Out of the spotlight the routine work continues. Grants are approved and the work supervised; buildings are inspected and their owners advised on repairs and alterations; applications for planning and listed building consents are processed; conservation areas are studied and improvements discussed and planned; the

THE ORIGINAL PEPPER STREET METHODIST CHAPEL, 'LOST' INSIDE A GARAGE SHOWROOM FOR HALF A CENTURY, NOW REVEALED.

H.R.H. THE DUKE OF GLOUCESTER OPENING THE RESTORED
KING'S BUILDINGS IN NOVEMBER 1985.

Programme is explained to visitors and students, and lectures are given to local groups. All these activities and many more are the essential underpinning of all the accolades and awards won by the City Council for its outstanding conservation achievement.

The successful restoration of Nos 2, 3 and 4 King's Buildings in November 1985 was an important moment for conservation in Chester. The buildings had been shored up for twenty years and the struggle to ensure their future had continued throughout the years of the Programme [see C.3.1]. His Royal Highness The Duke of Gloucester, Deputy Chairman of the Historic Buildings and Monuments Commission opened the completed scheme with these words:

The problem of making a city work is never a simple one. Many Councils send for the bulldozer but they pay the price in that they are less loved, less popular and more vandalised. What makes Chester different is the thought and care that has been put into it … it could not have come about without the support of the City Council.

Chester is in many ways a marker for the future. It is a success story. Today is a day for congratulations. First for the completion of this particular project but also for something of great significance. The City has been rewarded by success. People come from all over to see Chester and that brings the economic justification for the care taken. I am proud to be associated with this project and of part of the history of what has been happening here.

Chester is a wonderful example to others. It is a shame when people have to say 'Why didn't we do it like Chester'?

'THE FALCON' IN LOWER BRIDGE STREET,
ONE OF CHESTERS OLDEST 'BLACK AND WHITE' BUILDINGS.

NEW BUILDINGS IN WATERGATE STREET.

C

STUDY AREAS

Exactly the same thing is in being plonked down in town after town, the same sort

of supermarket beside the Cathedral

Richard Crossland,
Minister of Housing and Local Government
Chester Chronicle,
1966

Chester's face is its fortune', said the Insall Report, to which someone was heard to

add 'but some of her teeth are missing'. The skill of architects and

builders, engineers and planners have filled many of the gaps and, with the skill of

a dental surgeon, are preventing others from appearing.

C M Morris,
Director of Technical Services,
Chester Chronicle,
1974

C

STUDY AREAS

FOLLOWING THE broad outline of the Conservation Programme, this chapter considers a number of key areas, noting major achievements and identifying problems and opportunities for the future.

The Study Areas examined within the city centre are loosely based on some of the areas defined in the 1968 Insall Report. The last two areas show how the Programme has expanded to cover the whole of the district. The characteristics and problems of these areas vary widely, and this is also true of the Council's approach to finding solutions. In some areas it was the minutiae that needed attention, while in others a broad policy

of problems and solutions. Inevitably they include some of the most significant projects within the Conservation Programme, although some smaller, more typical, problems are also described. For example Nos 2,3 and 4 King's Buildings [see C.3.1] is the largest scheme tackled under the Programme with grants totalling over £300,000. In contrast the Oddfellows Hall [see C.5.1] has received a number of small grants over the years, ranging from £460 to £5,500.

C.1.0
THE ROWS

The Rows buildings and streets are the physical nucleus and the social heart

EASTGATE STREET SOUTH.

approach has produced the necessary improvements. Where confidence was particularly low the Council have had to step in and show what was possible; in other cases 'pump-priming' was all that was required. As confidence in the benefits of conservation has grown the general influence of the Programme has often been a sufficient stimulus. The one consistent theme is that conservation is a protracted, grinding task and requires patience and persistence to make things happen.

A number of case studies are included, describing in detail the Council's approach to particular problems. These have been selected to show a range

of Chester. The Rows themselves are a unique system of continuous covered galleries at first floor level. These galleries run above the shops at street level and are contained within buildings of various dates and architectural styles. This system survives along the four main streets that meet at the Cross, although it had previously been more extensive. It is the Rows that give Chester's shopping centre its distinctive character.

The Rows present a complete cross-section of the architectural evolution of Chester. They include many of the city's most important buildings and combine to form one of the best examples of historic townscape in the country. They form the

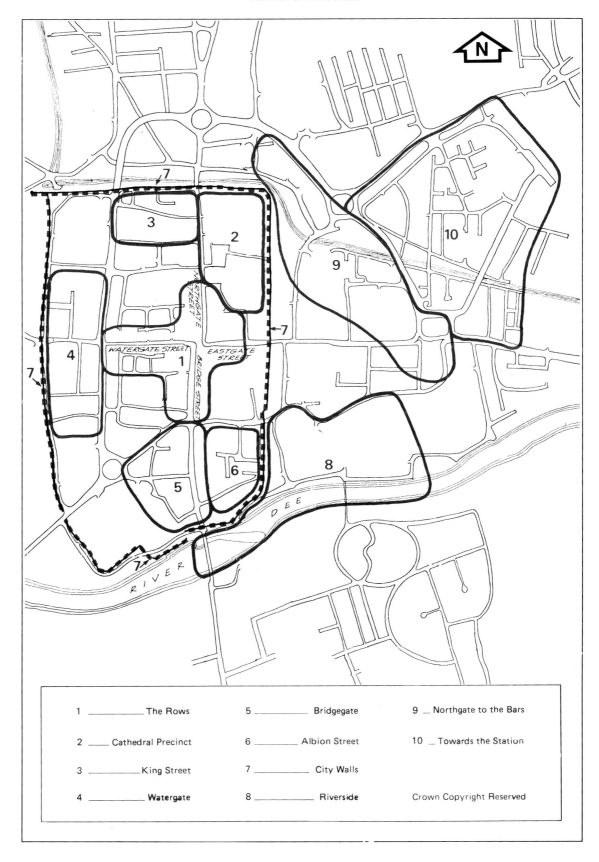

1 _____ The Rows	5 _____ Bridgegate	9 _ Northgate to the Bars
2 ____ Cathedral Precinct	6 _____ Albion Street	10 _ Towards the Station
3 _____ King Street	7 _____ City Walls	
4 _____ **Watergate**	8 _____ Riverside	Crown Copyright Reserved

commercial core of the city, and need to change and adapt in response to commercial pressures.

The Rows system often results in multiple ownership and tenancy of individual structures. This aggravates the difficulties of repair and maintenance, many people preferring 'not to know' about developing problems. The principal threat to the many of the buildings is the disuse of upper floors. There is little incentive to repair the whole of a building. It is more economical to maximise use of the street level and to abandon the remainder. The 1968 Insall Report noted that:

'The natural cycle of misuse, underuse and disuse, with subsequent decay, dereliction, demolition and finally redevelopment, is demonstrated in Watergate Street, and is also a problem in much of Bridge Street. If this process continues, large parts of the Rows will be redeveloped, and the historic attraction of the central area will rapidly wane'.

The report identified twelve Rows buildings with serious defects, fifty-seven that were deteriorating and only twenty in a satisfactory condition. It warned that there were buildings, '...where the mantle of prosperity is only skin deep. The mask could melt away with surprising speed if the underlying symptoms of decay are not soon remedied'. The consultants recommended: better maintenance, particularly of shared valley gutters between buildings; bringing upper floors into use; and a programme of improvements, including pedestrian bridges at Row level across the side streets. They also noted that:

'As a result of their policy of acquiring old property in the central area, the Corporation now owns several buildings on each side of Watergate Street ... It is tragic that having bought these historic buildings with the best intentions of conserving them, lack of suitable tenants and insufficient funds should have resulted in the loss of Nos 61-65 Watergate Row.'

Nos 61-65 Watergate Row and the adjacent building formed the notorious 'gap' site on the south side of the street. In the late 1950s some of the buildings were

LATE NINETEENTH CENTURY BUILDINGS AT THE CROSS.

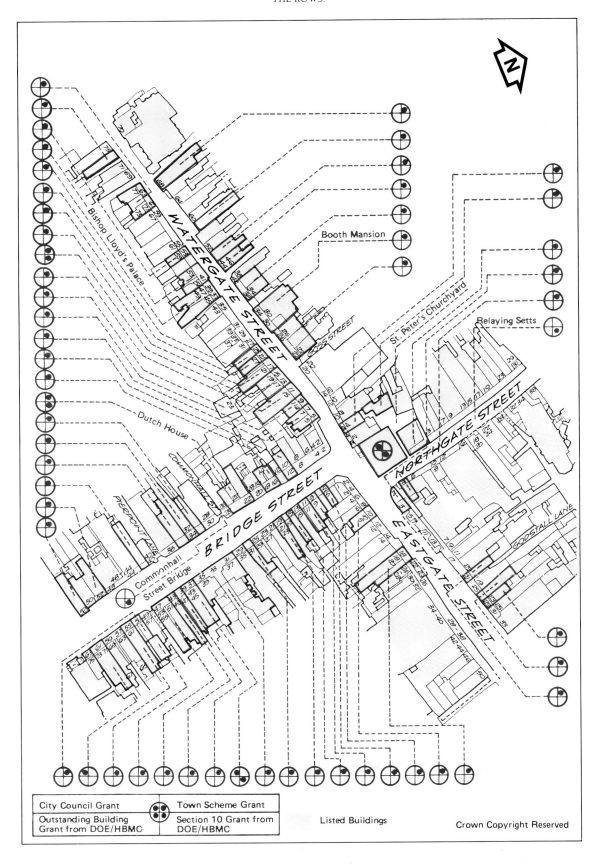

City Council Grant

Outstanding Building Grant from DOE/HBMC

Town Scheme Grant

Section 10 Grant from DOE/HBMC

Listed Buildings

Crown Copyright Reserved

demolished and the remainder were in such a poor condition that redevelopment was proposed. However no developer was interested in the site, and in 1961 it was decided to hold an architectural competition. The brief was for shops at street level with offices, storage and car parking above. A request from the Chester branch of the Council for the Protection of Rural England that flats should be included was rejected on the grounds that the site was unsuitable for residential use.

The winning design was announced in 1963, but still no developer was willing to undertake the scheme. In September 1965 the late Alderman P H Lawson submitted plans for the renovation of the eighteenth century building on the west side of the site. The City Engineer and Surveyor reported to the Improvement Committee that the Alderman's scheme was possible and would result in considerable savings, but that the restored building would not have as long a life as a new structure. The proposal was therefore rejected. By 1968 local feeling at the lack of any progress was very strong and the Council decided to develop the site itself, providing shops at street and Row level, with flats above. This proved a commercial success. Interestingly even today, almost two decades later, this site is still known locally as 'The Gap'.

During the early years of the Conservation Programme some small grants were given for repairs to Rows buildings; but the main activity was the restoration of the Dutch Houses [see C.1.1]. The one exception to this was the comprehensive restoration of 49 Bridge Street Row, at one time the rectory of St Michael's Church, which had serious problems with its timber frame. A scheme was agreed and grants offered by July 1973; but the owner died just as works were starting. Fortunately, the building was sold to the owners of a neighbouring property, who took over the whole of the restoration scheme.

St Peter's Churchyard, hidden behind the church, is a small public space surrounded by a variety of eighteenth and nineteenth century buildings. The whole area was semi-derelict, and the access

from Watergate Street Row was closed because of the danger to the public. It was agreed that the Council and the Department of the Environment would jointly cover the cost of demolishing two buildings, and that a third would be reduced in area. This work, together with associated improvements, was started in May 1974. Further environmental works and the restoration of adjacent buildings were carried out during subsequent years. As a result, a run-down corner of the city has been transformed into an inviting and well-used space.

One major obstacle to the economic success of the Row levels in Bridge Street and Watergate Street was the break in continuity at each side street. The 1964 Grenfell Baines Report had recommended pedestrian bridges to overcome this problem and in 1969 an application for the redevelopment of Nos 14-20 Watergate Street, immediately to the east of the junction with Goss Street provided the first opportunity. After extensive discussions with all interested parties a scheme was agreed. A similar arrangement became possible in 1971 when substantial alterations were proposed to No 40 Bridge Street, and the Council obtained agreement to bridge Pierpoint Lane. The final pedestrian bridge, over Commonhall Street, was erected in 1984 with the assistance of a Section 10 grant from the Department of the Environment.

During the early 1970s the Council became increasingly concerned about three of its properties on the south side of Watergate Street, including Bishop Lloyd's Palace [see C.1.2]. The restoration schemes prepared for these buildings included improvements to the residential units, demonstrating the potential of the upper floors of commercial properties. The work involved substantial disruption to parts of the Row, as some buildings had to be stored up and stretches of the Row walkway closed while repairs were in progress. The reorganisation of local government, together with financial restrictions, created some problems but work was completed in 1977.

Between 1978 and 1980, the Upper Floors Study was in progress; and to clarify the problem a pilot study was carried out in the block fronting Watergate Street and Bridge Street. This study recorded the uses and users of space, ownership and tenancies, access and circulation. It included the rear extensions, which in many cases were in the same empty and derelict condition as the upper floors. A detailed survey of all the buildings in the block was carried out, so that relationships between spaces, floor levels and access points could be determined. Detailed information enabled a very complex area to be understood, specific problems identified and solutions proposed.

The study led to an increased interest in the fundamental problems of many of the Rows buildings. During this period the leases expired on two Council owned properties on the north side of Watergate Street. These buildings were known to be in poor repair; and the Council's Property and Estates Committee decided to dispose of them on a long lease, on condition that they were restored and brought into full use. While this was being arranged, it was reported to the Development and Planning Committee that the buildings were deteriorating rapidly. That Committee therefore requested that some first aid repairs be undertaken prior to disposal. This was agreed, but some associated comments were not well received and the minute of the relevant Property and Estates Committee reads as follows:

Arising out of the discussion on the above properties at the meeting of the Development and Planning Committee, held on 5 September 1979, it was agreed that the attention of the Chairman of that Committee be respectfully drawn to the Gospel according to St Matthew, Chapter VII, verses 1 to 4 inclusive.

In September 1980 the Council decided to withhold part of the normal Town Scheme grant if there was no intention to use the upper floors. This has proved an effective incentive, encouraging owners to explore ways of making use of disused areas of their buildings [see C.1.3].

It has always been recognised that the public have a right of access to the Rows, and successive City authorities have been responsible for the management of the walkways, stalls, steps and bridges. Following Local Government Reorganisation in 1974, it was considered necessary to clarify the rights and responsibilities of all parties concerned with the Rows; and these are now specified in the Cheshire County Council Act 1980.

A three phase programme of repairs to the steps was undertaken between 1979 and 1982, half of the costs being covered by a Section 10 grant from the Department of the Environment.

During 1980, the owner of property on both sides of Godstall Lane enquired about the possibility of the surface of the lane being improved. At this time, Godstall Lane was an unattractive alleyway linking Eastgate Street Row North to St Werburgh Street. After some discussion, the owner agreed to carry out a scheme, using York stone paving and granite setts supplied by the County Council; the City Council making a grant towards the costs. Despite some last minute problems over additional costs, the City Council's unwillingness to increase its grant and the Department of the Environment's refusal of a Section 10 grant because of lack of funds for environmental schemes, the work was completed in 1982 and represented a substantial improvement. In 1983 the potential of the lane was realised by a local developer. He purchased a long narrow shop on the east side and an old warehouse on the west, converting them to form eight small shops with offices above. The warehouse had to be partially rebuilt and the opportunity was taken to provide an interesting modern facade. The whole scheme was imaginatively detailed, creating a high quality environment which received a Civic Award.

In recent years there has been pressure from some building owners to erect railings preventing public access to the Row stalls. This has been an understandable response to anti-social behaviour in some under-used sections of the Rows. In view of the historic public use of these areas, this expedient should be resisted. The best long term solution is to encourage more economic activity at Row level so that anti-social behaviour is discouraged.

The materials used for the Rows walkways and stalls are traditionally varied; timber, stone slabs and granolithic being most common, although one section is graced with the elegance of marble. Some recent refurbishments have replaced these traditional finishes with tiles or modern sheet materials, often carrying these through into the shop. This approach should be resisted; the walkways being defined as separate from the shop by its use of traditional finishes.

Although the general condition of the majority of Row buildings is now substantially better than the position reported in the 1968 Insall Report, the economic vitality of certain areas is still marginal. This is seen particularly in Bridge Street Row West and Eastgate Street Row North, but is generally true of many upper floors and rear buildings. It is important that the economic vitality of all areas be improved, so that the future maintenance of the buildings is assured. This can probably be best achieved by encouraging use of both the Rows and their rear buildings for small scale shops. These areas might also be improved by the use of more imaginative lighting.

Despite all the restoration work on Rows buildings, little research has been

THE DUTCH HOUSES IN BRIDGE STREET AFTER RESTORATION.

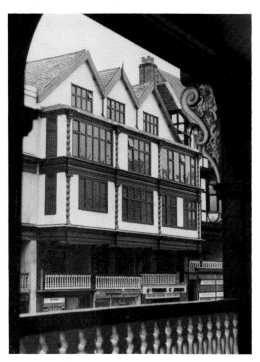

carried out on the origin and development of the Rows. In 1984, as part of the Festival of Architecture, an exhibition, 'Galleries which they call the Rows', was mounted at the Heritage Centre, and a day conference, 'The Rows of Chester', was organised by the Chester Archaeological Society. As a result of the interest aroused by these events, the City and County Councils established a Rows Research Project and, together with the Chester Civic Trust, funded a pilot study to stimulate interest in further research. This pilot study was completed during 1985, and funds are now being raised from a number of sources for a detailed investigation into the historic fabric of all the Rows buildings.

━━━━

C.1.1.
DUTCH HOUSES, BRIDGE STREET
A Problem of Joint Ownership.

The Dutch Houses are the most historically important buildings in Bridge Street, dating largely from the mid-seventeenth century. They have a very substantial jettied front above Row level, decorated with twisted columns and some fine internal decoration, including a magnificent plaster ceiling.

In 1968 over two-thirds of the buildings were empty or underused, and the whole block was deteriorating. In view of their importance, this was one of the first projects tackled under the Conservation Programme. The major problem was a division of ownership. The buildings divide naturally into three vertical blocks, each of which was separately owned. The matter was further complicated in 1970, when the owner of the central section sold the property at Row level and above to a fourth party, while retaining ownership of the shop at street level.

Following discussion with all the owners, it was agreed that the Council would commission an architect to carry out an appraisal. This was completed in July 1971 and indicated that the structure was in very poor condition and that immediate action should be taken to prevent it become dangerous. The report also recommended that the jettied front should be taken down and rebuilt with a very much reduced projection. The City Council accepted the principle of the report, agreed to grant aid repairs and attempted to bring the owners together for a joint scheme.

At first things went well. The three owners concerned with the upper floors of the buildings agreed to the principle of a joint repair scheme; and by February 1972 details had been agreed, including the restoration of the decorative ceiling. One problem was that the northern section was owned by Great Universal Stores; and as the Ministry of Housing and Local Government had stated in October 1970, '... the Minister's practice has been not to offer grant to commercial firms who could reasonably be expected to meet the cost of repair out of their own resources'. Eventually, it was agreed that the Dutch Houses were a special case and that the whole scheme would be grant aided. Meanwhile, preliminary investigations were undertaken, and a detailed repair scheme prepared for the front of the buildings.

However, by September 1972, the Council were becoming concerned at the delay in starting work, in view of both the deterioration of the facade and the increase in building costs. At a series of meetings with the architect and the owners over the following months, major problems developed. It became apparent that although the restored jettied front could be supported by the existing structure, this would not allow subsequent repair works to the central section of the buildings. It was suggested that the front should be provided with an independent steel structure, at an increased cost. Two of the owners claimed that they had been misled into thinking that the proposed repair scheme related to the whole structure, and not just to the front section. Meanwhile, the buildings had deteriorated to a point where temporary propping was required to prevent collapse.

As a result of these problems, the owner of the central section asked if the Council would purchase his property. As negotiations on this would take some time and the emergency repairs could not wait, he agreed to sign the contract for the demolition and temporary propping works on the understanding that the Council accepted liability for the cost of the removal of the decorative ceiling. This was agreed, and the work started on site in January 1973.

It soon became apparent that the demolition and temporary propping work were inadequate; and despite the introduction of additional dead shores the sandstone columns continued to move. The Building Inspector was concerned at the delay in reinstating the building and demanded further propping or demolition of the front section. After lengthy discussions, the owners agreed to the propping. This was carried out, but the scaffolding company then withdrew their guarantee for the dead shores because of the additional scaffolding that had been attached.

By early June 1973, a fixed price contract had been negotiated for the work and all three owners had tentatively agreed to proceed. However, the owner of the central section again asked if the Council would purchase his property. The Council agreed, on condition that the sale could be completed before the end of the month so as to secure the negotiated contract. This was achieved; the Council took over responsibility for one-third of the contract figure and work started on site at the end of July.

As soon as it was known that the Council had acquired the central section of the buildings, the owner of the southern section also asked it to purchase the part of his property above Row level. He had previously been negotiating with the owner of the central section, who had expressed a wish to purchase this part of the building, and without this sale he was unable to make his initial contribution to the scheme. The contractor immediately indicated that unless there were sufficient funds to meet his interim payments he would cease work on site. To allow time for negotiations over possible acquisition, the Council agreed to provide the owner of the southern section with a loan, to cover his payments to the contractor. The Council were unwilling to purchase only the upper floors of the southern section because of problems with access; but it did agree to buy the whole property, including the street level shop.

A second phase of work, securing the structural stability of the whole building, was agreed relatively easily between the two remaining owners. This was completed by January 1975, in time to win a Civic Trust Heritage Year Award. The Council completed work on the buildings with a third phase, consisting largely of internal works, designed to bring the whole building into use, and incorporating a flat in the top two floors of the building.

The Dutch Houses were saved. The Council's determination, flexibility and willingness to take over ownership produced the result after five years of problems.

C.1.2
BISHOP LLOYD'S PALACE,
WATERGATE STREET
Restoration of a Council Building

Bishop Lloyd's Palace, Watergate Street Row, consists of two seventeenth century houses, one of which displays the arms of George Lloyd, a Bishop of Chester. If the date of 1615 on the building records its construction, the Bishop cannot have lived there for very long, as he died in the same year. By the late nineteenth century the building was in a very poor condition and was in danger of 'removal'. In order to preserve the Palace, Alderman Charles Brown purchased it in 1899 and engaged the architect T M Lockwood to carry out extensive renovations. In 1938 the City Corporation purchased the adjacent buildings, receiving the Palace as a gift in 1948.

In 1970 the City Engineer and Surveyor reported on the poor condition of the Palace; and over the next few years a number of alternative uses were investigated. It was decided to start with repairs on No 51 Watergate Street, the property to the west. This was in a very poor state, the majority of the structural timbers being totally decayed, and with very little restraint or support for the front gable. The timber framed party wall to Bishop Lloyd's Palace had totally collapsed, due to water penetration through the valley gutter. As the tenant required modern shop and storeroom facilities, which could not be provided within the framework of the existing building, it was decided to build modern accommodation and to reinstate the front elevation. When this gable front was dismantled, evidence of an early timber frame facade was discovered. The new facade has been designed

BISHOP LLOYD'S PALACE, WATERGATE STREET.

using the details of this framing and the original bargeboards and carved bressumer have been reused.

While all this work was in progress, the fabric of Bishop Lloyd's was inspected in detail and some first aid repairs were carried out. During 1974 the Council decided to proceed with the second phase, involving a full restoration of the structure of the Palace and its conversion to provide shops, meeting rooms and a flat. During the restoration, it was discovered that some of the alterations carried out as part of the Victorian restoration had weakened the structure of the building. Both traditional and modern repair techniques were used to solve particular restoration problems. Decayed decorative timbers were replaced with hand carved copies and structural facade timbers were restored using polyester resin. Fine decorated ceilings were bolted back to the main beams and casts were taken of the plasterwork, in order to replace missing sections. The work was finally completed during 1977 and the Palace now provides the city with two delightfully unusual meeting rooms.

C.1.3
Nos 11, 13 and 15 WATERGATE STREET
An Upper Floor Success

Nos 11, 13 and 15 Watergate Street are a group of three Rows buildings. The street level of No. 11 consists of a fine thirteenth century crypt, but the rest of the building dates from the early eighteenth century. Although of less significance, Nos 13 and 15 are similar eighteenth century houses built above medieval structures.

In August 1979 a Town Scheme grant was offered for the reslating of the roof and other minor repairs to No. 11. This was part of a larger repair scheme, involving a number of other properties. During the course of the work, the rear wall of No. 13 was found to be bowing outwards. Although a short-term repair would have been possible, the aim was to bring the upper floors into use and it was decided to take down and rebuild the whole gable. This work also received a Town Scheme grant.

In November 1980 a schedule of repairs to the roof, gutters and chimneys of Nos 13 and 15 was agreed. A reduced Town Scheme grant was offered towards this work, because the upper floors would remain unoccupied after the repair. The owner was informed that the full grant would be paid if a scheme to bring the upper floors into use was prepared within two years. The repair scheme went ahead; a report on the feasibility of using the upper floors was produced and the full grant paid in October 1981. The report indicated that a new stair tower at the rear of No. 13 would provide independent access to the upper floors of all three buildings, but that no action could be taken until the expiry of current leases.

Early in 1982 a scheme was prepared for No. 11, where the lease had expired. The fine eighteenth century staircase could only be reached through the Row level shop unit; and the scheme proposed turning the lowest flight of this stair and separating it from the shop, so that direct access could be provided to offices and a flat on the upper floors. This meant losing almost a third of the shop frontage. Following discussions with the Fire Officer, consent was granted and a Town Scheme grant approved. Work started on site in September 1982, but during the following month the Fire Officer indicated that the scheme was inadequate for the purposes covered by the Fire Certificate. The main problem was the necessity of providing additional lobbies at first floor level. After a number of meetings, the Conservation Officer indicated that an application for listed building consent for the lobbies was likely to be refused. The Fire Officer then agreed to withdraw the requirement for lobbies and to accept the use of an existing escape route through the adjacent building.

In June 1984 a similar scheme to bring the upper floors of Nos 13 and 15 into use was prepared, in advance of a renegotiation

THE SEVENTEENTH CENTURY PLASTER CEILINGS IN BISHOP LLOYD'S PALACE DURING RESTORATION.

of the lease. This scheme involved the construction of a new staircase at the rear of No. 13, as had been proposed in 1981. General repair of the buildings was assisted by a Town Scheme grant, and the new staircase building received a Section 10 grant from the Historic Buildings and Monuments Commission. The scheme was completed in December 1985 as the first step in a long term proposal to establish a new pedestrian route through the backland area. Further progress towards this goal was achieved during 1986, when the thirteenth century crypt in No. 11 was converted into a wine bar. This involved the demolition of a derelict warehouse building, so as to provide a new rear access to the crypt. It is hoped that further small improvements in this area will encourage the reuse of adjacent derelict buildings and generate further progress in the rescue of decaying upper floors.

C.1.4

BOOTH MANSION, WATERGATE STREET
Restoration by a National Company

In 1700 George Booth reconstructed two medieval houses to form a new mansion, with the substantial frontage that we know today. Remains of the late thirteenth century houses still exist within the building, which is listed Grade II*. Later it became the Assembly Rooms; and after the Second World War was used by the College of Further Education and then by the Public Analysts Department. The 1968 Insall Report observed that the laboratories and offices of an institutional character were quite alien to the architecture of the building.

By 1976 Booth Mansion was partially empty and in a state of accelerating decay; the complex roof being in a very bad condition and the elaborate cornice sporting vegetation. The building was on the market, the owner having failed to implement a 1973 planning permission for a new five storey block at the back of the building, which would have provided a total of 13,000 square feet of offices.

The building was sold and the new owner agreed to carry out essential repairs before a new use had been found. The first phase, the reslating of the roof and repairs to the cornice, was completed by the end of

1977. A second phase included selective demolition and making good at the rear. All this emergency work was supported by the Council and the Department of the Environment through a Town Scheme grant.

Early in 1978 the new owner decided not to develop at the rear, and later that year it was announced that the building was to be taken over by Sotheby's as a regional saleroom. The Council and the Department of the Environment agreed to waive their rights to reclaim the Town Scheme grant, because of the particular circumstances of the change of ownership.

Further substantial repairs, together with extensive improvements, had to be carried out before the building could be brought back into use. An application for Section 10 grant from the Department of the Environment was refused because of the large financial resources of the applicant's parent company. A subsequent application for grant assistance from the Council was also refused, the decision being explained in the following letter:

I regret to inform you that at the meeting of 31 January 1979 the Development and Planning Committee resolved that in view of the considerable financial aid already given towards the repair of this building, and in view of limited resources now available, your application for additional grant aid should be refused. I should stress that, unlike the Historic Buildings Council, the City Council do not consider the financial status of the applicant to be a major determining factor unless available funds are at an extremely low level, in which case the Development and Planning Committee may have to judge which of many schemes under consideration would benefit most from grant aid, and the likelihood of certain schemes being implemented without public support.

Despite this lack of grant the restoration scheme proceeded, being completed in July 1980. Booth Mansion is now a busy saleroom, providing an unrivalled setting for an international business.

C.2.0
CATHEDRAL PRECINCT

The Cathedral precinct is a large self-contained area, screened from the bustle of the city centre by the bulk of the Cathedral to the south, and enclosed to the north and east by the City Walls. The formal terraces, handsome town houses, enclosed gardens and cobbled streets create an atmosphere of restrained elegance. To enter Abbey Square from Northgate Street, through the momentary darkness of the Abbey Gateway, is a dramatic transformation to quiet; with cobbles underfoot, grass and trees, in an architectural enclosure of Georgian nobility and Cathedral grandeur.

The area is largely owned by the Dean and Chapter of the Cathedral and they face considerable problems in maintaining such a large group of historic buildings in addition to the cathedral and its monastic structures. The 1968 Insall Report identified serious defects in six buildings, three of which were considered to be incapable of economic use, and a further twenty-one that were deteriorating. Behind the principal frontages there was an unsightly muddle of decayed outbuildings and derelict land.

THE COBBLED STREET SURFACE WITH YORK STONE CARRIAGE 'WHEELERS' IN ABBEY SQUARE.

The eighteenth century street surfaces, which are included in the List of Buildings of Special Architectural or Historic Interest, were threatened by lack of maintenance and excessive car parking.

The Insall Report proposed the redevelopment of much of the Abbey Green area to provide new shops and maisonettes on the Northgate Street frontage with new town houses behind. In 1973 the Dean and Chapter produced an outline scheme for redevelopment of this area; including a five storey office block adjacent to the Northgate, to finance the residential element and the restoration of the adjacent listed buildings. Following the preparation of a planning brief by the Council, which placed a number of restrictions on the proposed development, it was agreed that a comprehensive study of the whole Cathedral precinct was required in order to assess the implications of the redundant playing fields, the increased number of listed buildings and the changing uses of the buildings around Abbey Square. Unfortunately the Dean and Chapter were not in a position to finance such a study.

The archaeological importance of the Abbey Green area was well known; and in view of the proposed redevelopment, an excavation of the area adjacent to the City Walls was started in March 1975. As a result of the discovery of important sections of the Roman rampart and associated buildings, the whole of the open area in the north-east angle of the City Walls was scheduled as an Ancient Monument. This was a further restriction on any new development. A further draft planning brief was prepared by the Council proposing the retention and repair of all listed buildings and Nos 128-132 Northgate Street, which it had previously been planned to demolish. It also recommended that the quarry area should be used for car parking [see C.2.1], as considerable foundation problems could be anticipated if any development was undertaken there. Substantial new development was still envisaged within the Precinct. The discussions on this draft brief continued for three years.

In the meantime, the Dean and Chapter were offered their first Town Scheme grant in 1972 for the rebuilding of the gable wall of No. 6 Abbey Square. A later grant for the reroofing of the houses on the north side of the Square was made conditional upon the reinstatement of the window glazing bars, the removal of which had damaged the scale and integrity of these imposing terraces. The result is an handsome improvement to their appearance.

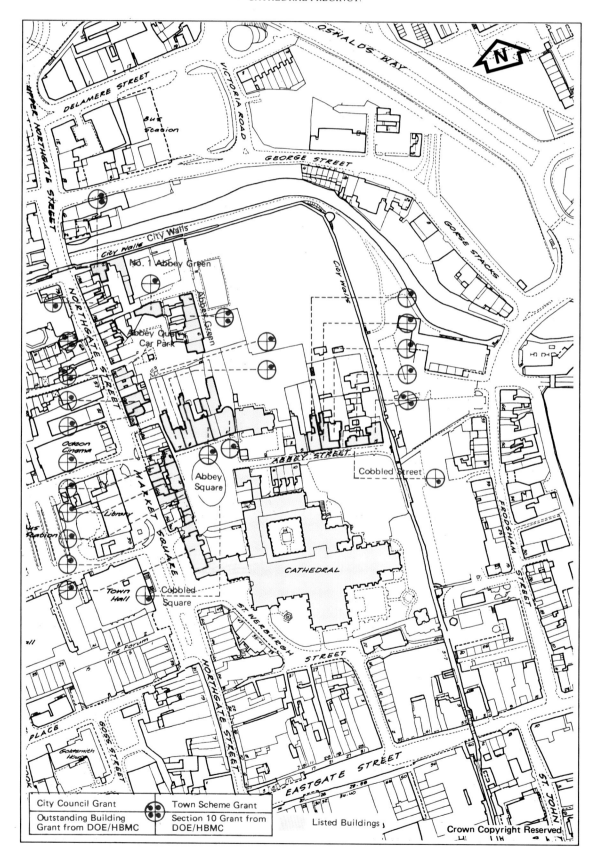

City Council Grant	Town Scheme Grant
Outstanding Building Grant from DOE/HBMC	Section 10 Grant from DOE/HBMC

Listed Buildings

Crown Copyright Reserved

Despite these repairs in Abbey Square and an agreement that the buildings around Abbey Square could change to predominantly office use, five years of discussion had failed to make any significant progress on the fundamental problems of the Cathedral Precinct. Three groups of buildings owned by the Dean and Chapter were in such a poor structural condition that they were given first priority status in the 1976 Review Study. One of the major difficulties was that the income from the Precinct is essential for the long term maintenance of the Cathedral, and therefore the sale of buildings could not be considered. Equally, there were insufficient capital resources to embark on the major restoration programme that was required.

The appointment of a new Dean in April 1978 proved to be a turning point; and a gradual programme of repair and improvement was started. By the end of that year, plans were in progress for the Abbey Quarry Car Park [see C.2.1], the restoration of No. 1 Abbey Green, the display of the excavated Roman buildings and the repair of the historic surface of Abbey Street. The Abbey Street scheme was assisted by a 50% Section 10 grant from the Department of the Environment and an additional grant from the Council, covering 25% of the extra cost of using a specialist contractor for the relaying of the cobbles. In 1981 a similar repair scheme of the surface in Abbey Square was undertaken, but with a smaller proportion of grant.

Unfortunately, the proposals for the Council to take over No. 1 Abbey Green and create a permanent display of the Roman buildings failed to materialise because of shortage of funds. The excavated structures were covered with sand, and No. 1 Abbey Green continued to deteriorate. In 1980 the occupant of No. 1 and 2 City Walls, an interesting pair of houses built immediately adjacent to the City Walls, came to a tentative agreement with the Dean and Chapter about the possibility of a long lease for the buildings, and commissioned a feasibility study. This study was grant-aided by the Council and the Department of the Environment, and

ABBEY SQUARE.

led to their restoration with the help of Housing Improvement grants and a substantial Town Scheme grant.

During the same period the Dean and Chapter carried out substantial repairs to the roof and chimneys of Abbey Green Terrace, a fine eighteenth century group overlooking the playing fields. This work received a Town Scheme grant; and the oppportunity was taken to reinstate the traditional form of sash windows, to relocate a conglomoration of waste and soil pipes from the front elevation to the interior, and to repair the boundary walls. This additional work received a Section 10 grant from the Department of the Environment.

By 1983 the Dean and Chapter had given up any idea of being able to redevelop their Northgate Street buildings. As part of their consultancy, Donald W Insall and Associates prepared a report on Nos 122-138 Northgate Street, which demonstrated that the shops could be improved and the upper floors brought into full office and residential use. The principles of this report were adopted; and over the next two years the leases were renegotiated to allow the first phase of work to proceed. This has now been completed with the benefit of a Section 10 grant, and it is hoped that the second phase, which involves improving the access to the upper floors, will start in the near future.

The buildings of the Cathedral Precinct are now in a relatively sound condition, with the major exception of No. 1 Abbey Green. Continuing repairs will aways be necessary; and further work to improve the economic use of all the buildings may be appropriate. This may be assisted by the fact that the Dean and Chapter generally take a different view of time scale and financial return than most owners. In view of the importance of the open spaces of the Precinct some environmental improvements deserve consideration, such as the repair of the cobbled surface of Abbey Green and the restoration of the railings to the centre of Abbey Square. The idea of exhibiting the Roman buildings in Abbey Green might well be reconsidered given the increasing emphasis on tourism.

C.2.1
ABBEY QUARRY
An Alternative Place for Cars

Behind the fine eighteenth century buildings of Abbey Square and Abbey Green is an old quarry, which is thought to have provided the stone for some of the buildings in the cathedral precinct. The area was

ABBEY GREEN TERRACE.

occupied by a range of mews buildings and a number of semi-derelict timber sheds, and the northern part had been used for the tipping of builder's rubble.

In a Development Brief for the Cathedral Precinct [see C.2.0], agreed between the Council and the Dean and Chapter, the area was allocated for a car park. This was intended to produce substantial improvements to the quality of the area, and was linked to an agreement to reduce the number of vehicles in the adjacent Abbey Square, a fine eighteenth century space marred by a congestion of parked cars.

In September 1978 Donald W Insall and Associates produced a report for the Council, outlining a plan to create this new

car park. The Dean and Chapter agreed to proceed on this basis, and the first phase was implemented during 1979. This involved the demolition of all buildings and walls within the area, removal of the spoil heaps to create a level site and the provision of a hardcore base for the parking area. This work received a 50% Section 10 grant from the Department of the Environment.

The second phase of work involved the surfacing of the car park, landscaping, repairs to adjacent walls and improvements to the access road. After resolving a number of minor problems, such as a small land exchange and the replacement of a deteriorating stone building, a major difficulty appeared in the form of unexpectedly high tenders. A full 50% Section 10 grant was not available, and the Dean and Chapter were seriously concerned that the car park scheme was proving too large a commitment and that their limited resources might be better concentrated upon repairing their

building stock. The Council agreed to a grant to make up the shortfall, but declined to provide a loan in addition. The work proceeded on this basis, being completed during 1981. The end of the scheme was marred by problems over the continued existence of a small area of builder's rubbish which detracted from the improved appearance of the area. After a two year correspondence over the matter, the lack of action led to part of the Council's grant being withheld.

The new car park accommodates thirty-five cars in a pleasant backland space, and has allowed a reduction in the number of cars using Abbey Square. Thus two areas have been improved, as a result of the one scheme.

C.2.2
NO 15 ABBEY STREET
Using Every Available Grant

No. 15 stands at the end of Abbey Street, immediately adjacent to the City Walls, and is of particular visual importance as it has three prominent elevations. The eighteenth century facade is a refronting of a seventeenth century house, which appears to have been constructed over an earlier stone structure, while the back dates from the nineteenth century. Even when the structure was totally stripped down during restoration, it proved impossible to identify clearly the historical development of the structure.

In 1968 the Insall Report had indicated that the building was deteriorating, and in 1973 an engineer's report was commissioned and the possibility of using the building as a new Deanery was discussed; but no progress was made. By 1976 its condition was so bad that it was given first priority status. There were active structural movements, leaking rainwater pipes and a defective roof. The building was considered to be beyond economic repair.

In 1980 the Dean and Chapter were encouraged, by the offer of 75% grant aid from the Council and the Department of the Environment, to commission an architect to report further on the condition of the building and to advise on its future use. This report identified differential settlement, failure of bonding between external and internal walls, cracked foundations, displaced and bulging brickwork, inadequate roof structure and general deterioration of all external elements. The building had provided eight 'bed-sitters' with shared bathroom and kitchen facilities, and the report recommended conversion to six self contained flats. The first floor reception room in the rear wing created some problems, as the architect reported:

There is a large room - too large for the requirements of an ordinary flat and if retained as one room would be an uneconomic use of space. It also has some attractive architectural features in the triple arched north window and gothic side window, and the large fireplace, which are very fine in the context of a large reception room but inappropriate in the smaller rooms of a conventional flat.

It was proposed that this room should be converted into a studio flat by introducing a sleeping gallery at one end. This arrangement, together with some other aspects of the proposals, were felt to be unsympathetic to the interior features; and a revised scheme providing four larger flats was approved in November 1982.

The repair work needed was very extensive and substantial grant aid was necessary. A special combination of Housing Improvement grants, a Section 10 grant and an additional grant from the Council proved necessary to make the scheme economic. The contract extended over twenty months during 1983 and 1984. Part of the work involved the taking down and rebuilding of the whole of the north gable with its

ARCHED WINDOW AT 15, ABBEY STREET.

fine gothic arched window, a major feature of the building when seen from the City Walls. Unexpected structural problems during the work resulted in substantial additional costs and the conservation grants were increased. Despite these problems, the scheme has been successfully completed and provides attractive homes in a superb location.

—

C.3.0
KING STREET

King Street is the best of Chester's minor historic streets. It slopes down from Northgate Street, with continuous frontages behind narrow pavements, following a gentle curve and giving constantly changing vistas. It contains a fine mixture of eighteenth and nineteenth century houses, mainly small, but often with good interiors. The finest group is King's Buildings, which stands at the western end, close to the Inner Ring Road.

The 1968 Insall Report noted that the street suffered from strong external pressures. To the north, the Northgate Brewery dominated visually and generated unpleasant smells and substantial heavy traffic. It also owned a number of tied cottages on the north side of the street. Commerce House, a large modern office block to the south, dominates and overshadows the houses; and is an unfortunate object lesson in relations between new and old. As a result of these problems and a pattern of absentee landlords, eighteen properties in the street had serious defects and a further eleven were deteriorating. Despite this large scale decay the report recommended that:

The residential character of King Street should be strengthened by all possible means. This will mean combining uneconomically small units and reconditioning others. For

houses backing on to the Northgate Brewery, especially where rent-controlled, this may not for some time be possible. It is meanwhile important that they should not be allowed to deteriorate any further.

Within months of the publication of the report, the Northgate Brewery had closed, equipment was removed and the buildings left in a semi-derelict condition. In October 1969 the Council received a letter from the Brewery surveyors:

The demolition of the houses fronting King Street would enable the building line to be set back thereby providing for the future widening of King Street [although we appreciate that this is contrary to the views of the Insall Report]; any new buildings fronting King Street could then be designed in such a way as to be in keeping with the present character of the street.

At this time none of the houses in the street, apart from King's Buildings, were included on the statutory List of Buildings of Special Architectural or Historic Interest, but the resurvey of the city was in

KING STREET.

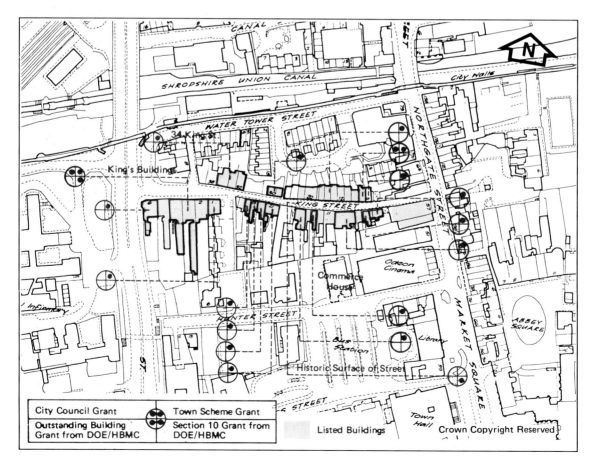

City Council Grant	Town Scheme Grant
Outstanding Building Grant from DOE/HBMC	Section 10 Grant from DOE/HBMC

Listed Buildings   Crown Copyright Reserved

progress. King Street was also being considered as a possible pilot project, following the publication of the Insall Report. The Council exchanged a number of letters with the Brewery stressing the importance of the King Street houses. In reply the Brewery stated a wish to co-operate with the Council, but felt that the future development of the site was being handicapped by uncertainty over King Street.

While discussions were in progress on the acquisition of the Brewery by the Council, to enable the implementation of a primarily residential development, the site was sold to a private development company in January 1970. After extensive discussions, the Council agreed to a scheme which retained and renovated the King Street houses, developed the north-east section of the site with a major office block and provided a small block of new housing on the north-west section. The scheme included the former Fire Station building in Northgate Street and the associated firemen's cottages which were owned by the Council. The planning approvals were phrased in such a way as effectively to prohibit the occupation of the office block until a substantial start has been made on the restoration of the King Street houses.

The Brewery site was of substantial archaeological interest and the developer agreed to demolish the buildings to allow time for a major investigation. Archaeological excavations extended over a number of years and produced substantial evidence of the Roman fortress and the subsequent development of the area.

DERELICT COTTAGES IN KING STREET, JUNE 1982.

HOUSES IN KING STREET DURING RESTORATION.

During the early 1970s there was some progress in the rest of King Street. Discussions had started on King's Buildings [see C.3.1], work was in hand on an extensive restoration of No. 21 and the owners of Nos 1 and 3 were considering a scheme to renovate their properties. Nevertheless, despite the stated good intentions of all parties, no substantial progress was being made on the major problems. The low environmental standard of the area, together with an application for a five storey office block at the west end of the street, led to the formation of the King Street Area Residents Association in 1974.

By early 1975 the developer of the Brewery site was in difficulties. The builder of the office block had gone into liquidation, and no start had been made on the restoration of the houses. As a result, the half completed office block was taken over by another company and the houses were sold to the building contractor who had submitted the lowest tender for their restoration. The City Council and the Department of the Environment transferred the agreed package of grants to the builder and agreed to waive the normal condition on the repayment of grants in the event of the properties being sold. In order to guarantee the restoration of the houses, which had previously been covered by the conditions on the planning approvals, an agreement under Section 162 of the Housing Act 1974 was made between the Council and the builder.

Work finally started on the restoration of these thirteen houses on the north side of the street in July 1976, but it proceeded very slowly, not being finally complete until June 1980. This extended period of disruption inevitably created concern and friction. One resident described King Street in 1979 as a 'building battleground', with the front of his house being '...assailed by vehicles trying to squeeze between our wall and the invariable truck parked opposite....'.

At the same time restoration work was also going on elsewhere in the street, a further eleven properties receiving grant aid between 1972 and 1982. Unfortunately, the work was not always to a satisfactory standard. In April 1978 Donald Insall commented in some surprise on the

THE FINE ENTRANCE TO NO. 3 KING'S BUILDINGS WAS IN VERY POOR CONDITION.

HOUSES IN KING STREET.

fact that No.34 King Street had been rendered. The Conservation Officer replied:

I agree that normally this practice is not one to encourage but in this circumstance there was no alternative. The building had previously been 'repointed'. In fact there was mortar everywhere - the building had the apperance of being repointed with a spade rather than a trowel!

As the various restoration works in the main stretch of King Street were completed, there was substantial pressure for environmental improvements. The 1976 Review Study recommended that detailed proposals should be prepared for traffic management and environmental improvements in the street. There was also pressure for a residents parking scheme, but that was resisted by both the County Council, as highway authority, and the police.

At a meeting between the King Street Area Residents Association and representatives of the Council in June 1981, the idea of removing the tarmac surface and reinstating the setts and York stone paving, first floated ten years earlier, was discussed. The first phase of a scheme covering the majority of the street was agreed, divided between the two financial years 1982/83 and 1983/84. A Section 10 grant from the Department of the Environment was conditional upon a substantial proportion of the work being completed by 15 March 1983. This deadline proved impossible to meet, because of the need to renew a water main in the street, but the

Department agreed to pay the grant in respect of the stone setts purchased for the scheme. The work was completed in November 1983, with only one change in the historic pattern of wheelers and setts. At the same time new wall-mounted street lights were installed. It is hoped that the second phase of the scheme, which was not possible until after the completion of the restoration of King's Buildings, will be carried out shortly.

The future of King Street as a fashionable residential area is now secure and changes are likely to be minimal apart from two problem areas at the western end. The site at the rear of Nos 5 and 6 King's Buildings is still an eyesore and needs to be developed with new housing, while the future of the block in front of King's Buildings is uncertain. This end of the street would be greatly enhanced by the addition of some trees. A residents parking scheme is still needed and a new traffic circulation pattern for the area, involving one-way streets, could reduce the impact of vehicles.

―――

C.3.1
NOS 2,3 and 4 KING'S BUILDINGS
It takes a long time...

King's Buildings is a terrace of Georgian houses, designed on a bold scale with grand staircases and fine interiors. During 1964 the Council became aware that there was substantial movement in the front wall of Nos 2, 3 and 4 as a result of settlement in the foundations. The owners, who used these houses and No. 5 as a men's hostel, would not consider carrying out the necessary repairs. After extensive discussions, it was agreed that permanent raking shores would be erected to support the front wall. This was achieved in 1965, after some difficulty in obtaining the size and quality of timber required.

The 1968 Insall Report noted that the terrace needed urgent repair and commented that, 'The stately rooms of King's Buildings deserve a more worthy use than the flatlets or institutional quarters into which some are divided'. Early in 1972, a package of grants and a loan were agreed for a scheme estimated at £45,000. For the next two years little progress was achieved, despite regular threats by the Council. By June 1974 working drawings and Bills of Quantities had been completed and the estimated cost had risen to £83,000. The Department of the Environment then expressed concern at the total costs and requested a reduced scheme to tie the building together, rather than to take down and rebuild the front wall.

During the next two years there were further discussions on a repair scheme, on the need to carry out works so as to obtain a fire certificate and on the possibility of the owners buying some Council owned land at the rear. By the summer of 1976 it was evident that the condition of the houses was steadily deteriorating. There were new cracks in the brickwork and window glazing; and the raking shores were no longer supporting the front wall.

In April 1977 the Council served a Dangerous Structure Notice under Section 58 of the Public Health Act 1936 and also threatened to serve a Repairs Notice under Section 115 of the Town and Country Planning Act 1971. The Council were anxious to avoid demolition and, as it was clear that the owners were unlikely to meet any costs of repair, the only alternative was Council acquisition. This could not be considered without substantial financial support from the Department of the Environment.

In May 1977 a structural report commissioned by the Council stated '...there had been a recent acceleration of movement...' As a result, alterations and repairs were made to the raking shores, and scaffolding was erected to provide further sup-

NOS. 2, 3 AND 4 KING'S BUILDINGS BEFORE RESTORATION.

port for the front wall. This work was financed by the Council and the Department of the Environment. At the same time a feasibility study on the future of the buildings was commissioned, which stressed that very substantial grant aid would be required to make the restoration of the buildings an economic proposition.

Following the service of a Repairs Notice in 1978, the Council opened negotiations for purchase and also started discussions with a number of developers who were interested in the restoration. It was hoped that a developer would buy the buildings direct from the owners, but this would mean that the Department of the Environment could not provide a grant towards the cost of acquisition. Negotiations continued for two years while the buildings continued to deteriorate, the Council having to carry out further works to prevent collapse in 1978 and 1979. By November 1979, Members of the Council were expressing concern at the continuing cost of hiring the scaffolding. This had not been purchased in 1977, because the repairs had been anticipated in the near future. Two years later the position was rather different, but as the scaffold company were not prepared to sell, there was no alternative to paying the hire costs until a repair scheme could be started.

By October 1980, it was obvious that no progress was being achieved through negotiation, and the Council served a new Repairs Notice with a view to proceeding to compulsory acquisition of the properties under Section 114 of the Town and Country Planning Act 1971. The owners said that they would repair No. 5, but could not afford any of the work necessary on Nos 2, 3 and 4. In order to maintain their business, they also asked if an exchange of Nos 2, 3 and 4 for other property owned by the City would be possible.

During the first half of 1981 four separate activities were in progress; compulsory purchase proceedings, negotiations with the owners on a possible exchange of properties, discussions with interested developers and a regular weekly inspection of the buildings to monitor their deterioration.

The owners objected to the compulsory purchase order, but also began discussions on a possible extension behind No. 5 to compensate for the loss of Nos 2,3 and 4. The Council rejected this idea on the grounds of over intensive development, but agreed to sell some land at the rear of No. 5, thus making possible a separate residential development. As a result, the owners agreed to sell Nos 2,3 and 4 to the Council without the need for compulsory purchase.

In the meantime the Council had agreed the principles of an agreement with a developer for the future restoration of the buildings. This involved the demolition of the rear extensions and conversion into twelve flats, with a new rear access and parking on land owned by the Council. This scheme was not considered financially viable with normal levels of grant aid. By May 1982 an 80% Town Scheme grant was

agreed, together with a Section 10 grant from the Department of the Environment for demolition and enhancement work. The Department also agreed to give a grant towards the cost of acquiring the buildings, which the Council would transfer to the developer. As the basis of the scheme was that the developer would sell the flats, the Department and Council agreed not to enforce the normal condition on the reclaim of the grants if the properties were sold within a three year period. In return, the developer agreed to accept a fixed profit margin; any balance being made over to the grant giving bodies.

The complicated legal agreements necessary to implement the scheme were drafted during May 1982. Lengthy discussion then followed to finalise the details of the property transfers, access rights, parking arrangements, party walls, drainage, alternative fire escape arrangements, levels of grant and the allowable profit margin. After a year of negotiations the agreements were finalised, but at the last moment the owners declined to sign, because of reservations about the valuation of the properties by the District Valuer. As a final gesture of goodwill the Council agreed to allow the owner's agent to confirm with the District Valuer the principles upon which the valuation would be established. This was subject to a condition that the agreement be signed within seven days of that confirmation or the Council would proceed with the compulsory purchase. The agreement with the owners was finally signed on 13 October 1983.

The Council acquired Nos 2, 3 and 4 King's Buildings on 26 July 1984; and eleven days later sold them to the developer. Work started immediately on clearing out the buildings. The main remedial work involved the rebuilding of virtually the whole of the front wall. Before this could be undertaken, the floors and roof had to be supported with internal propping so that the external shores could be removed. This entailed the casting of a 'temporary' reinforced concrete beam, 0.6 metres wide, 1.5 metres high, 22.8 metres long, in the basements to provide a solid base for the support system. Once the front wall had been taken down, a similar beam was cast alongside to provide the foundation for the rebuilt wall.

This complex restoration project was finally completed in November 1985; and the quality of this fine terrace of houses can once again be appreciated, after being hidden behind massive timber shoring for twenty years. However, it is clear that the long delay in achieving restoration resulted in substantially increased costs which were largely met by central and local government.

C.4.0
WATERGATE

The Watergate area is a self-contained enclave cut off from the city centre by the inner ring road. It has a very mixed character with some handsome Georgian buildings alongside a variety of post-war developments. Despite the major traffic routes of Nicholas Street and Lower Watergate Street, the general feeling is one of peace and quiet.

The 1968 Insall Report noted very mixed use of the area, with a corresponding variety in the condition of the build-

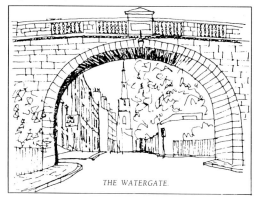

THE WATERGATE.

ings. Few properties were empty, but many were underused and in a poor state of repair. Thirteen buildings had individually serious defects, while a further twenty-nine were deteriorating. Two major development opportunties were identified; the Linenhall Stables, and an underused area between Nuns Road and Nicholas Street Mews. In June 1975, planning permission was granted for the erection of 76 flats on this latter site, but problems with the acquisition of the whole area meant that the scheme was abandoned.

The 1976 Review Study highlighted the number of deteriorating buildings, indicating that little had been achieved in

this area during the first five years of the Conservation Programme. Two blocks of buildings were given first priority status, with fifteen second priority and a further twelve third priority status. The study recommended consideration of the problems of the Stanley Place/Lower Watergate Street area. Almost every building on the north side of Lower Watergate Street was deteriorating and there were problems with traffic noise and vibration, car parking, and the development of rear gardens. A similar study of the rear of the Nicholas Street terrace was also recommended.

In February 1976 an inspection of Greyfriars House and Blackfriars House was carried out by architects acting for the majority shareholders of the company who owned both buildings. These two houses form a single block dating from the eighteenth and nineteenth centuries, incorporating a timber-framed building of the sixteenth century. The architects became so concerned that a joint inspection was carried out by the Building Inspectors, Environmental Health Inspectors, a Fire Officer and the Conservation Officer. The architect's report of that meeting lists structural defects in the roof timbers, a serious fire risk because of the layout and construction of many of the partitions, the general lack of kitchen, bathroom and toilet facilities, and a general state of disrepair. One of the inspectors confirmed:

...that it was not practicable to carry out the work necessary to make the building habitable and to comply with the various Fire and Housing Regulations.

An application to demolish Blackfriars House and replace it with offices was submitted, but after two years of negotiation the proposal was withdrawn. Both buildings were then sold, and Greyfriars House was gradually improved and extended. Similar work to Blackfriars House is still awaited. Over the past ten years the Council has considered ten different schemes for a variety of work to these buildings, most of which have involved processing both planning and listed building consent applications.

City Council Grant	Town Scheme Grant
Outstanding Building Grant from DOE/HBMC	Section 10 Grant from DOE/HBMC

Listed Buildings

In October 1979 the semi-derelict condition of Nos 88-90 Watergate Street was drawn to the attention of the Council, who agreed to the service of an Urgent Works Notice under Section 101 of the Town and Country Planning Act 1971. The property was eventually sold and fully restored with the help of a substantial Town Scheme grant. The scheme also involved the erection of a replica eighteenth century building to replace the single storey garage on the corner of Watergate Street and Stanley Street. Over the past six years, a further six properties on the north side of Lower Watergate Street have received Town Scheme grants, and that area is slowly improving.

The Greater Chester Local Plan stressed the importance of retaining and encouraging residential uses in this area. There is pressure to convert the remaining flats in Stanley Place, Watergate Street and Nicholas Street to offices, but the Plan states that part of the building, particularly the upper floors, must be retained for residential use.

During 1980 a study was commissioned of No. 93 Watergate Street, a late eighteenth century house owned by the Council. It was in a very poor condition, with serious deterioration of the slate roof and the brickwork. Early in 1982 the tenants were rehoused, and in view of the cost of repairs it was decided to offer the property for sale. When no reasonable offers were received, it was suggested that the house was unsuitable for residential use because of traffic noise and the lack of a garden. The Development and Planning Committee did not consider these to be adequate grounds for varying the Local Plan policy for the area, and firmly resisted the idea of office use for the whole of the building. After further advertisement of the property one offer was received, but this failed when it was realised that the proposal involved the erection of an external fire escape stair. After two and a half years on the market, the building was sold to a Housing Association who converted it to a hostel for homeless men.

In February 1982 planning permission was granted for a sheltered housing scheme on part of the underused area between Nuns Road and Nicholas Street Mews. Both before and after the submission of the scheme, there were discussions on the form and detail of the design, because of the prominent nature of the site in relation to the City Walls. It is hoped that the garage in Nicholas Street Mews, adjacent to this site, will become available for a further residential development in the near future.

This area has steadily improved over the past ten years, but it still has a somewhat 'tatty' appearance. The Council have recently proposed a block restoration scheme for Nos 4-28 Nicholas Street, a prominent eighteenth century terrace, partly aimed at upgrading the external appearance. This is being supported by a Section 10 grant from the Historic and Buildings Monuments Commission. A similar scheme would be appropriate in Lower Watergate Street, in conjunction with environmental improvements to Stanley Place.

C.4.1
NOS 1 AND 3 NUNS ROAD
Restoration versus Home

Nos 1 and 3 Nuns Road are two early nineteenth century houses that look out across the City Walls to the racecourse. No. 1 is a simple cottage, probably incorporating an earlier building, but No 3 is a very pleasant Regency house with some good internal features. They are both listed Grade II.

In September 1977 the owner applied for listed building consent to demolish on the grounds that the houses were in a very dilapidated condition. At that time the upper floors of No 3 were occupied, but the

rest was empty. There was substantial local objection to this application, from a strong feeling that the owner had deliberately allowed the property to deteriorate. The Council refused consent, and the owner then appealed against this decision.

Before the appeal had been determined, the Council resolved to serve a Repairs Notice under Section 115 of the Town and Country Planning Act 1971; but agreed to hold this in abeyance until the outcome of the appeal was known. During 1979 the Council granted an outline planning approval for sheltered housing on an adjacent site, and this included the use of Nos 1 and 3 Nuns Road as staff accommodation. In January 1980 the Secretary of State dismissed the appeal against refusal of consent to demolish, stating that '...in all the circumstances, it would be premature at this time to permit the demolition...'.

Following this decision the Council reactivated the Repairs Notice and also served an Urgent Works Notice under Section 101 of the Town and Country Planning Act 1971. As a result, certain repair works were carried out by a new owner, primarily to the roof of No. 1; but these were of a temporary nature. The new owner indicated that he wished to carry out a full restoration scheme, but was having difficulty in obtaining access to the occupied section of No. 3. The occupant, a single lady, was not prepared to leave her home and had no faith in the intention to restore the houses. Despite regular correspondence, there was no progress for a further two years. By this time the conditions for the occupant were very bad; she had no electricity or heating and had to obtain water from another part of the building. She also looked after a large number of cats, which was to lead to complaints from neighbours in the adjacent new development.

There was a very extensive outbreak of dry rot in No. 1, and in October 1983 the Council served a second Repairs Notice on both houses. The schedule of works attached to this notice had been carefully prepared, so that it would be possible for the works to No 3 to be carried out with the occupant still in residence. The two months period allowed in the Repairs Notice expired; and a letter from the owner's

NOS. 1 AND 3 NUN'S ROAD.

solicitor stated:

Our client company never has, and does not now consider it practicable to carry out any works to the property with the tenant in occupation.

Your Council may be assured that the property will be restored as soon as practicable.

The Council responded:

Your assurance that the properties will be restored 'as soon as practicable' is, with respect, of little comfort to the Council, as if the present 'impasse' as regards the tenant is not resolved, it is unlikely that there will be anything left of either property worth restoring.

In March 1984 the Council decided to start compulsory purchase proceedings, and the owner then agreed to prepare a scheme of repair and rehabilitation. The compulsory purchase was deferred, subject to compliance with a tight timetable for the necessary approvals and for the start of work. Applications for planning permission and listed building consent were approved, tenders received, and a Town Scheme grant offered. The owner then again indicated that he considered it unrealistic to carry out the work while the building was occupied, and that he would not seek the necessary court order to obtain possession. When the Council insisted that compulsory purchase would proceed unless work started immediately, the owner agreed to open negotiations for the Council to purchase the buildings. After a further eighteen months, the sale was completed.

Although the Council now own the houses, the difficulty with the occupant remains. She does not wish to move. The Council do not have the resources to carry out the restoration and therefore wish to sell the property with vacant possession. Legal action appears to be inevitable.

———

C.5.0
BRIDGEGATE

The 1968 Insall Report noted that the Bridgegate area was '...one of Chester's worst examples of area decline, and a solution is urgent.' This encouraged the Council to give the area priority; and as a result of seventeen years of intense activity the picture has been transformed. The buildings are in good condition, gap sites have been developed, there is an air of prosperity and it is now an attractive area for investment.

The story of the Bridgegate Action Area has been published in 'Conservation in Action - Chester's Bridgegate' [HMSO 1982]. This section does not duplicate that report, but brings the story up to date.

In the late 1970s and early 1980s, Nos 26-42 Lower Bridge Street were the major blot on the Bridgegate success story. The site had been subject to an outline planning permission for comprehensive redevelopment, but no action had been taken. In 1971 No. 30 had to be demolished; and in 1973 the Council expressed concern at the condition of the remaining buildings. The owners did not consider

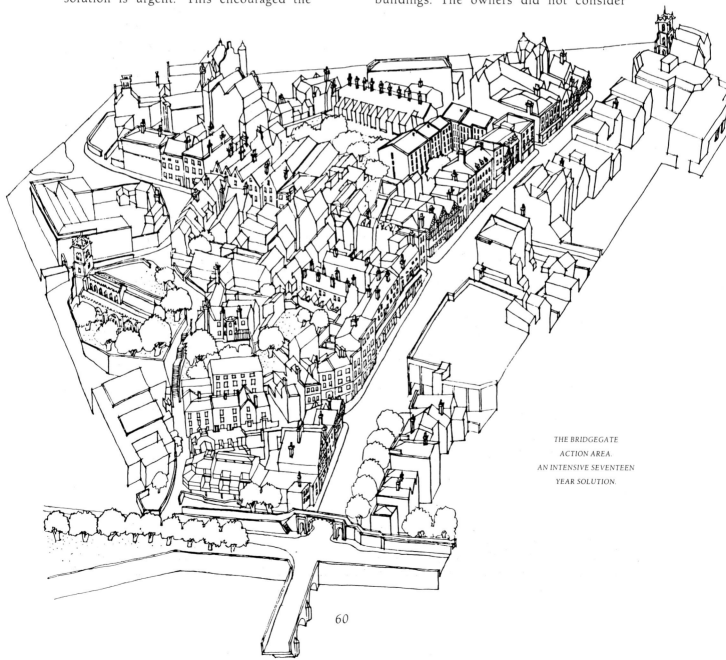

*THE BRIDGEGATE
ACTION AREA.
AN INTENSIVE SEVENTEEN
YEAR SOLUTION.*

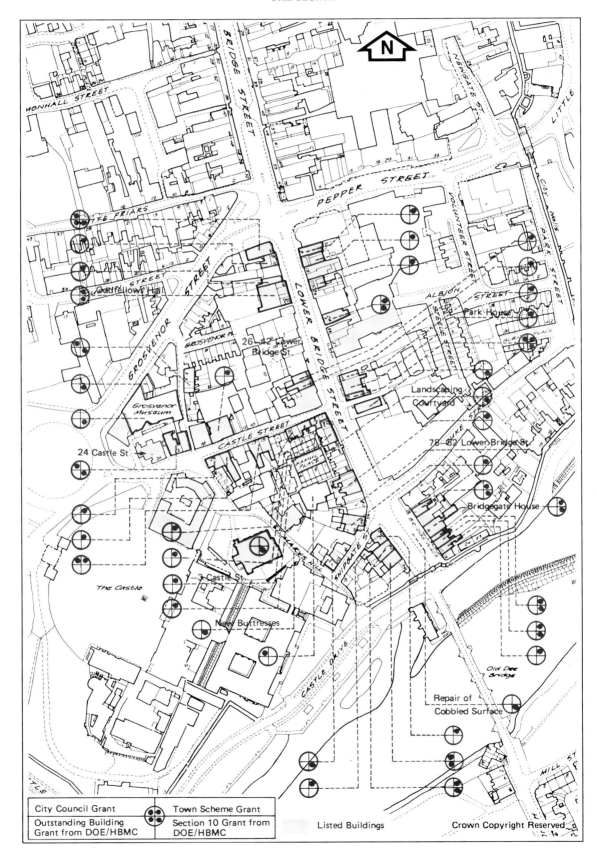

them to be in a dangerous condition, despite the fact that the top floor of No. 42 had collapsed. The following year, a detailed development proposal failed when the owners became bankrupt; and in February 1978 Nos 34-42 were demolished as unsafe, while a public inquiry into their demolition was actually in progress. The inquiry was both predictable and disappointing. Donald Insall commented:

...the result of the inquiry seemed so indeterminate and offered such weak support for the City in requiring reinstatement as a condition of any planning consent. With the best will in the world, it is difficult for any architect to design a new complex with a long frontage, which would take its place between Chester's narrow, broken street sub-divisions.

The Greater Chester Local Plan identified the resulting site as suitable for residental, office or hotel development, but required that the front facades of Nos 34-42 should be rebuilt. In May 1980 a planning application for a hotel was submitted, recreating these facades and providing a 'modern' infill on the site of Nos 26-30. After extensive discussion on the detailed design, this was approved in May 1981, but the scheme failed to go ahead because of an increasingly depressed hotel market. In February 1982, a change to offices within the shell of the approved

design, was agreed, and this led to the scheme that was actually built, ten individual office buildings set around a courtyard. The Council insisted on the inclusion of shops along the main frontage and housing in Castle Street. This scheme recreated the eighteenth century facades and completed the street scene with a neo-Georgian infill.

A redevelopment scheme for Nos 78-82, Lower Bridge Street had been approved, subject to a condition that the front facade should be retained. In November 1983 the developer started to demolish this facade. The Council immediately obtained an ex parte injunction restraining the company from carrying out any further unauthorised demolition. This proved to be a highly effective measure, allowing time for the future of the wall to be properly considered. Consent for demolition and replica rebuilding was eventually approved; but at the subsequent court hearing, the company pleaded guilty and were fined £250.

The restoration of other buildings has continued. After the City Council had threatened to serve a Repairs Notice under Section 115 of the Town and County Planning Act 1971, Bridgegate House, an important eighteenth century house in Bridge Place, was sold by the County Council. The new owner is carrying out an imaginative refurbishment, with a Town Scheme grant towards the structural repairs and a Section 10 grant, from the Historic Buildings and Monuments Com-

GAP SITES AND DERELICTION ON THE WEST SIDE OF LOWER BRIDGE STREET IN THE LATE 1970s.

ODDFELLOWS HALL,
LOWER BRIDGE STREET.

mission, towards the cost of a new stair tower that allows access to the upper floors. Nos 17-19 Lower Bridge Street have been repaired with a Town Scheme grant, and the upper floors, which had not been occupied since the First World War, have been brought back into use as flats. Nos 1-3 Castle Street, the structural condition of which had been a matter of serious concern, have been restored. The owner of these buildings was able to demonstrate that the scheme was uneconomic without a higher than usual grant, and a 75% Town Scheme grant was therefore agreed.

No 24 Castle Street, a fine early nineteenth century building, had been disfigured by some flat roofed additions to the front elevation. The Council purchased the building, retained a strip of land to give rear access to the Grosvenor Museum, and then sold it, on condition that the original architectural form was restored. This restoration should be completed next year. The Council have been similarly anxious to see the development of the remaining gap site in Lower Bridge Street, adjacent to Park House. An outline approval was recently granted for hotel development, incorporating Park House. It is hoped that this will proceed in the near future.

As a result of all this conservation activity, the once dilapidated buildings of the Bridgegate are today generally sound; and the area is full of vitality and confidence. There remain opportunities for enhancement, by putting in hand various detailed environmental improvements. In particular the pavement surfaces and street furniture could be improved, and the later tarmac surfaces of many of the small streets, such as Bunce Street and Castle Street, might be stripped off to return them to their attractive earlier textures. Meanwhile, the accelerated return of life to the area, the variety of its rapidly reviving shops and the increasing demand for new and improved housing, gives the Bridgegate a lively and very remarkable character within the walled City.

CONSERVATION ACHIEVEMENTS IN THE BRIDGEGATE AREA
WERE RECOGNISED IN 1983 WITH THE AWARD OF A
EUROPA NOSTRA MEDAL.

C.5.1
ODDFELLOWS HALL, LOWER BRIDGE STREET
Little and Often.

The Oddfellows Hall, formerly known as Bridge House, was built as the handsome early eighteenth century town house of the Williams of Bodelwyddan. The lower floor has since been altered to form shops, but there are many good interior details, including a number of panelled rooms.

In November 1973 the owners, The Independent Order of Odd Fellows, Manchester Unity Friendly Society, Loyal City of Chester Lodge, were offered a small Town Scheme grant for repairs to the roof and remedial work to some panelling in one of the principal rooms. The roof repairs were completed, but the Lodge was not in a financial position to carry out the work to the panelling. By 1976 the condition of the building was beginning to be a matter for concern. The Review Study identified it as a third priority building; and at a working party meeting it was reported to be '...inadvisable to walk on the carpet, as it is highly dubious as to what is underneath it...'.

During 1982, a series of reports indicated an extensive outbreak of dry rot in the front of the building, affecting areas of the timber panelling. There were also problems with window lintels and one of the main beams. Remedial work, including the reinstatement of the panelling, was carried out with the help of a Town Scheme grant.

The experience of this repair work convinced the Lodge of the need to institute a programme of repairs. A report on the condition of the whole building was commissioned and necessary works were identified. During 1985 the roof and chimneys were repaired, and in 1986 the brickwork on the south elevation was repointed, together with repairs to the windows and rainwater goods. Both these phases of work received Town Scheme grants.

Further work will be needed in the future, particularly on the west elevations, and it is hoped that this can also be supported with a Town Scheme grant. When the owner of a large and complex building has limited financial resources for repair,

THE NORTH SIDE OF SHIPGATE STREET BEFORE
RESTORATION AND REBUILDING STARTED.

the temptation is to do nothing. By encouraging the Lodge to continue with a programme of regular repairs, the future of the Oddfellows Hall can be assured.

C.5.2
SHIPGATE STREET
New and Old Revive a Street

Shipgate Street is a short and attractive street with a cobbled surface, set just within the City Walls. Together with St Mary's Hill at its western end, it has a smallness of scale which gives this corner of the City its own distinctive character. Shipgate House, at the corner with Lower Bridge Street, is a handsome early eighteenth century house, and the other buildings form a very attractive group.

Along with the rest of the Bridgegate Area, Shipgate Street suffered neglect during the immediate post-war years. In particular, during the early 1960s the County Council was purchasing properties in anticipation of having to extend County Hall as far as the west side of Lower Bridge Street. The 1968 Insall Report identified three buildings with serious defects and two more

that were deteriorating. Only one of the historic buildings in the street could be described as being in fair condition. The general deterioration of the area was so advanced that the Report suggested substantial sympathetic redevelopment to bring it back to life.

During 1969 and 1970, discussions were held with the County Council about the future of the area. The City Council indicated that some redevelopment for County Offices might be acceptable, provided this was 'domestic' in scale, but the demolition of major historic buildings, like Shipgate House, would be resisted. Despite the fact that these buildings had originally been purchased for demolition, the County's policy was reversed; and 1971 saw the first phase of the restoration of Shipgate House and its adjacent cottage.

The 1973 Interim Bridgegate Report indicated that the County Council were still investigating the possibility of redeveloping the majority of Shipgate Street to provide for their increasing office requirements. In view of the deteriorating state of the buildings on the south side of the street, the

---

THE MODERN DEVELOPMENT ON THE SOUTH SIDE OF SHIPGATE STREET AS SEEN FROM THE RIVER.

report recommended that if a practicable scheme has not been produced within twelve months, the City Council should proceed with the compulsory acquisition of these properties and produce their own scheme for the redevelopment of the area. No progress could be made on a scheme, and following the threat of compulsory acquisition, the City's purchase of the buildings on the south side of the street was successfully completed in 1973.

Despite this change of ownership, little initial progress was made because of a conflict of policies between the two Council's. The 1976 Review Study commented:

The stalemate now existing demands a postive and realistic policy for the area. From an economic, logistic and environmental viewpoint, further extension of County Council offices into the area seems unlikely. During the past five years considerable changes in emphasis have taken place within the whole area, and the consolidation of existing residential development has been secured. It is recommended that the principal land use for this area be residential, with ancillary office and commercial use - e.g. professional offices on the ground floor with living accommodation over.

Where possible, the first objective should be to rehabilitate existing buildings; but in certain circumstances the interest of the area may be better served by sensitive redevelopment.

No progress was made for some time, but in 1978 the County Council offered to provide a footpath from the foot of St Mary's Hill to the riverside at Castle Drive. It was also agreed that a report on the potential of both sides of the street should be prepared by Donald W Insall and Associates as part of the consultancy arrangements. This report, completed by November 1978, suggested that eight residential units could be created on the north side. This involved the conversion of Nos 6,8 and 10, a replica rebuilding of No 12 which had substantial structural problems, and the addition of two new houses on St Mary's Hill. On the south side total clearance and redevelopment was suggested except for the facades of Nos 3 and 5, which were to be incorporated within a design for eleven residential units with some car parking. An interesting element of the proposed new development was that, by agreement, it could be cantilevered over the County Council's parking area, taking full advantage of the magnificent views over the river. This report proved acceptable to both Councils; and in 1979 it was agreed that the City Council would acquire the County's properties on the north side of the street to enable the scheme to be implemented.

In view of the near ruinous condition of Nos 3 and 5 Shipgate Street, their facades were shored up to prevent collapse before work could start. This work received a Section 10 grant; but as a result of further delay these buildings became so dangerous that they had to be demolished in 1981.

By this time it was agreed that the only way forward was to advertise the availability of both sides of the street, and to see if anyone would be prepared to carry out residential schemes. By April 1982, the City Council had acquired all the problem properties on the north side of the street, and was able to advertise them for sale. Simultaneously, both Councils jointly marketed the south side for residential development. One developer was successful in obtaining both sites, and negotiations started on new design proposals. These involved retaining Nos 6, 8 and 10 as houses, a replica rebuilding of No 12 to provide three flats, and a new house on St Mary's Hill. On the south side, a frankly modern scheme for seventeen flats and maisonettes was produced above a new underground car park. Work was finally completed in 1985, without any grant aid. After years of neglect and decay, Shipgate Street is once again an attractive place in which to live.

———

C.6.0

ALBION STREET AREA

This neighbourhood, tucked into the south-east corner of the walled city, is a quiet backwater of houses, apparently remote from the commercial activity of Chester. In the 1960s when the commercial centre was expanding, the area appeared to offer potential for redevelopment. Clearance proposals threatened and little maintenance or improvement work was carried out.

The 1968 Insall Report noted that Duke Street was '...a most pleasant and well-used corner, eloquent of the advantages that could result from future domestic use in favoured sites within the walled city'. It also noted that the nineteenth century terraced cottages were at the end of their life, and therefore proposed redevelopment with flats and maisonettes.

As a result of this policy, homes deteriorated. Nos 32-38 Duke Street, which had been 'listed' in 1972, were demolished by the Council as sub-standard, after efforts to rehabilitate them had been thwarted by restrictions in local authority expenditure. Other houses had been demolished earlier as part of proposals for widening Duke Street and putting a new road through the Territorial Army Drill Hall. These demolitions destroyed the townscape of the upper end of the street, a quality which the recent housing development is beginning to restore.

Meanwhile, the Council were determinedly resisting the pressures of commercial development spreading south across the ring road; particularly the idea of a pedestrian bridge across Pepper Street from the Grosvenor Precinct.

An increasing appreciation of the value of retention and renovation gradually reversed the clearance policy; and in 1979 the area was included in a programme of housing rehabilitation. The Council also decided to adopt policies that would safeguard the Victorian character of the neighbourhood. Home improvement schemes often result in 'modernisation' of the outside appearance of houses, destroying the consistent quality and character of an area. The location of Albion Street within the City Walls justified the establishment of a special scheme, complementing the internal

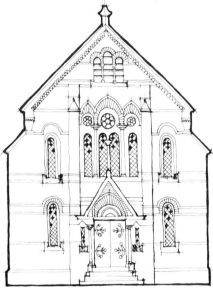

THE WELSH CONGREGATIONAL CHAPEL, ALBION STREET.

improvements with restoration of the original external appearance.

The Albion Street Housing Action Area was declared in April 1981 covering 69 houses. With the agreement of the residents a package of associated measures were adopted. An Article 4 Direction was approved by the Secretary of State, enabling the Council to control minor external alterations, including painting. A design guide was produced for owners, explaining features and details which were important to the character of the houses. As a result of the Article 4 Direction and the design guide a five year Section 10 scheme of grants from the Department of Environment was negotiated, ensuring that residents and owners would not have to bear the additional cost of restoring the external features. These grants were calculated to reflect the additional costs of using historic materials and details, supplementing the Housing Act grants.

In 1984, the average cost of a full improvement and restoration scheme on a single house in the Action Area was around £16,000, with an average Section 10 grant of approximately £2,000.

A number of properties had been improved before the scheme started. In some of these houses, features such as doors and windows had already been altered. The Section 10 grant scheme, together with matching grants from the Council, encouraged the owners of these properties to reinstate the original features. In two cases this involved building 'dummy' chimney stacks to maintain the skyline appearance.

Nos 1-23 Albion Street, a terrace of twelve small Victorian houses typical of the area, were in a desperate state. The rear half of the terrace had subsided over a long period, resulting in severe internal cracking and dragging the roof away from the chimneys. The Council's consultant

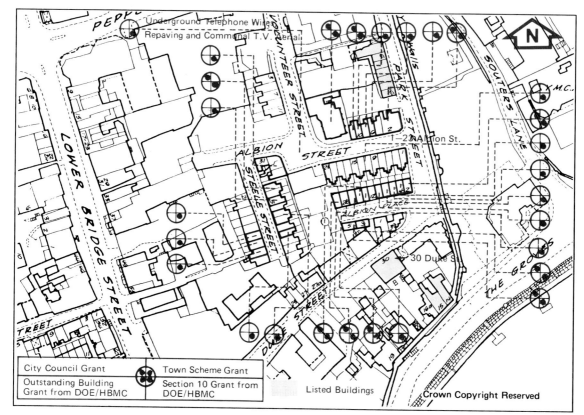

City Council Grant | Town Scheme Grant
Outstanding Building Grant from DOE/HBMC | Section 10 Grant from DOE/HBMC
Listed Buildings | Crown Copyright Reserved

structural engineers reported that the cost of the necessary rebuilding far exceeded the vacant, improved value of these properties. Acquisition for clearance seemed the most likely solution, but this would have undermined the policy for the area.

A feasibility study was carried out and after a great deal of further investigative work it was decided the rehabilitation might be possible, if tackled as a single contract with substantial grant aid. Organising the scheme became the problem. Discussions with the owners floundered and only when the Council resolved to compulsory acquire the seven privately-owned, tenanted properties, were negotiations for a voluntary sale speedily concluded. These seven houses and the one vacant property were acquired by a

Housing Association, which also acted as agent for the four owner occupiers.

The scheme involved the demolition of the outriggers, the rear wall and all the yard structures; a new rear wall was constructed and the interiors were reorganised to provide new kitchens and bathrooms. Although this reduced the size of the houses, the owners and tenants found that the provision of modern facilities far outweighed the disadvantages. The restoration of this terrace, which is now the centre-piece of the Albion Street Housing Action Area, was made possible as the result of a substantial Section 10 grant from the Historic Buildings and Monuments Commission.

The twin social centres of the Victorian community have also been

TERRACED HOUSES IN ALBION STREET.

included in the general enhancement of the area. The Albion Public House has had its original appearance restored by its brewery owners, encouraged by a token conservation grant. In particular, external pipes have been removed from the front and etched glass reintroduced into the windows. The Welsh Congregational Chapel had been struggling with a small congregation for many years, and was in a poor state of repair, with extensive dry rot. Part of the church had been used by the St John Ambulance Brigade, who purchased the building in 1985 and carried out an extensive repair scheme with the help of a Section 10 grant. The intention is to convert it into a first-aid training centre, with exhibition and lecture rooms.

When the Housing Action Area was declared, the residents identified use of the streets for general city centre parking as the main environmental problem. Unfortunately it has not been possible to introduce a residents' parking scheme [see D.3.4]. The funds available for environmental improvements have been concentrated on restoring the original appearance of the streets. With the help of Section 10 grants, pavement surfaces have been restored with original materials and a communal television aerial has been installed. The undergrounding of telephone wires and the restoration of the street surfaces are also planned. When the Drill Hall was sold for a housing scheme, part of the site was retained by the Council for the creation of a small public garden.

The whole area has now been renewed and revitalised. This has been achieved through the detailed and daily mangement provided by the Council's Action Area co-ordinator. The nineteenth century cottages have been improved and

their original character restored. This quiet backwater is once again an attractive residential area, '...eloquent of the advantages....' of living within the walled city.

———

C.7.0
THE CITY WALLS

Chester's major historic feature is the red sandstone wall which runs for almost two miles around the heart of the city. It was originally built by the Romans during the second century, but has been extended, realigned and rebuilt on innumerable occasions.

The nature of the Walls has meant that repair and maintenance has been a constant preoccupation for the city over the centuries. The 1968 Insall Report noted a number of places where strengthening was required and recommended regular replacement of individual worn stones, careful repointing, and the use of natural stone paving instead of concrete paving slabs. The report also recommended a number of improvements relating to access, lighting and the clearance of redundant buildings to allow better views of the Walls.

During the early 1970s no substantial repairs were carried out, but in 1973 the five principal Gates were cleaned as part of 'Operation Eyesore'; and Morgan's Mount, a small tower on the north wall, was repaired. By this time it was clear that certain areas of stonework needed comprehensive repair. The Water Tower and adjoining Spur Wall were identified as priorities and, following discussions with the Ancient Monument Directorate of the Department of the Environment, the first phase of repairs was started in 1975. Six yew trees, which had been planted on top of the wall, were removed and the stonework of the southern half of the tower was consolidated or rebuilt. Work to further sections was carried out over a number of years, being completed in 1984.

A comprehensive report on the condition of the Walls was submitted to the City Council in 1976 and provided the basis for a capital programme of repairs, with grant aid from the Department of the Environment. This recommended the re-

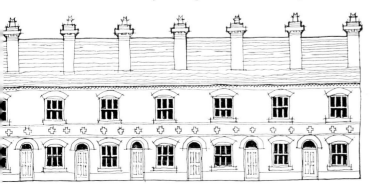

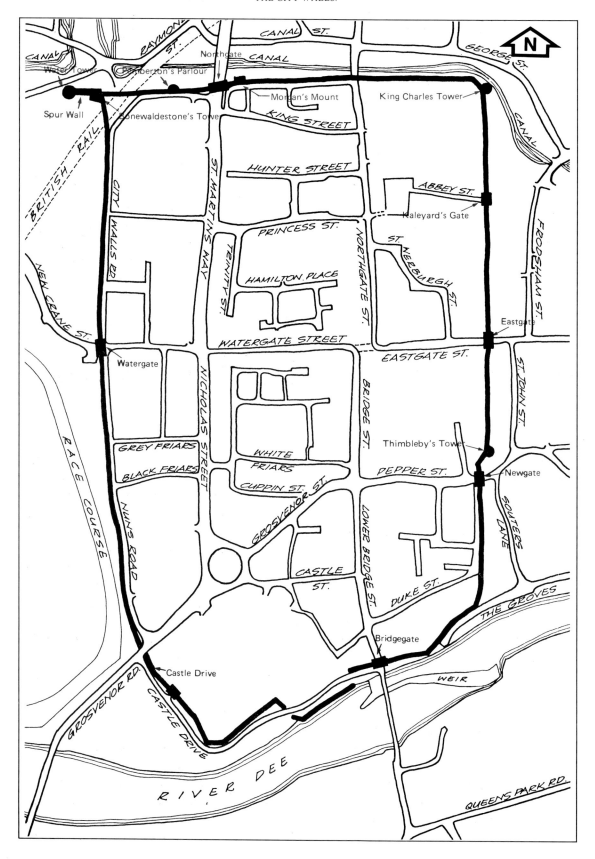

moval of trees and shrubs which were damaging the stonework, investigation of the condition of the stretch north of the Kaleyards Gate, and urgent repairs to Thimbleby's Tower and to the parapet above Castle Drive.

In the following year work was in progress on Thimbleby's Tower, where much of the stonework had to be renewed, and on the Castle Drive parapet, where the Victorian repairs had left the bedding planes exposed so that the stone had exfoliated to a dangerous condition. At this time the Conservation Area Advisory Committee published a report on the environmental problems of the Walls and surrounding areas. The Council had already purchased a number of properties between the north wall and the canal; and this area was improved during 1977 and 1978 by the clearance of sheds, the regrading of the bank and the provision of new gates.

In 1978 extensive repairs were started on King Charles' Tower, in connection with its use as a small museum focussing on the Civil War. The roof construction of this tower is unusual, with overlarge timbers set out like the spokes of an umbrella, and extensive repairs were necessary to the wall-plate in addition to the renewal of all the slates and leadwork. It was previously known as the Phoenix Tower and the remains of a stone tablet carved with a phoenix can be seen on the west side. During the repairs it was decided to provide a new weathervane, and the design represents a phoenix rising from the flames.

In the same year, structural movement was unexpectedly identified in a section of the Walls to the west of the Northgate. Fears of collapse led to the closure of a length of the walkway so that investigations could be undertaken. Paving stones from the top of the wall were lifted and a bulging section at the base was opened up. It was found that the loose core material in the centre of the wall had shifted, leaving substantial voids below the paving and at the base. This core was consolidated, the voids were backfilled, and the base of the wall was reconstructed.

KING CHARLES' TOWER.

The structure of the Walls, two skins of stonework with loose core material between, makes them particularly susceptible to this type of problem. The increasing use of the Walls walkway is almost certainly resulting in vibration, which causes the core material to shift position, creating voids. The movement of various stretches of wall is now accurately monitored in an attempt to identify problems before they require urgent attention.

General repairs to the north wall, between the Northgate and King Charles Tower were carried out during the winter of 1981-82. The fact that this stretch of wall stands on the edge of the sandstone cutting of the Shropshire Union Canal, made it necessary to scaffold from the canal tow path some fifty feet below. This substantially increased the costs of what was otherwise a relatively straightforward repair. Unfortunately that winter was unusually severe and the location was so

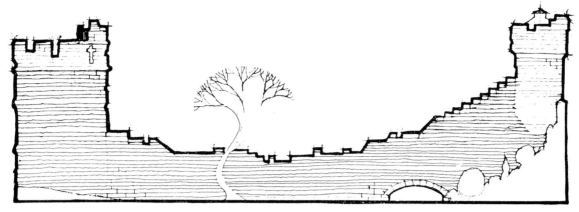

THE SPUR WALL BETWEEN THE WATER TOWER AND BONEWALDESTHORNE'S TOWER.

cold and exposed that the masons compared it to the north face of the Eiger. While the scaffolding was in position the opportunity was taken to carry out a detailed archaeological investigation of the external face of the wall. Also a section of the interior was examined and a small excavation carried out at the base.

In 1982 work was required to the wall immediately north of the Kaleyards Gate. The inside face of this section had been leaning for many years, but measurements showed that the movement was beginning to accelerate. The loose core material was excavated, the two skins of stonework tied together with stainless steel rods and the core replaced with grout.

In addition to these major projects various minor repairs were carried out during the late 1970s and early 1980s. Stone balusters on the Bridgegate and Watergate were renewed, the roof of Bonewaldestone's Tower was replaced and repairs were carried out to the stonework and roof of Pemberton's Parlour. A number of environmental improvements were also achieved, particularly along the canal, and new steps near the Kaleyard Gate, to provide access between the wall walkway and the towpath, were constructed with the help of a Section 10 grant.

Since April 1983, the City Council have acted as agents for the County Council for the paving and railings on the Walls, some sections of which require annual attention as a result of the sheer numbers of people who use the walkway. The County Council still retains respon-sibility for the lighting on the Walls; but it might be appropriate for the City Council to take this on a similar agency basis, so that all the work on the City Walls can be co-ordinated by one authority.

In recent years 'local' red sandstone has become a scarce and valued material. The Council try to maintain a stock of reclaimed stone, but it is difficult to obtain the quality and size required and occasionally new stone has to be used.

All the Council's work on the City Wall has been carried out in collaboration with the Ancient Monuments Division of the Department of the Environment, and now the Historic Buildings and Monuments Commission. Meetings are held with their inspectors, architects and engineers to discuss repairs and agree specifications. The Council is particularly grateful for the financial support provided by the Commission for the repair programme. In 1981, a 25% grant of up to £30,000 was offered for work over the following ten years, and this was not limited to a specific sum in any one financial year. This flexibility has been very helpful.

The majority of recent work has concentrated on the north and east sections of the Walls. General repairs and repointing are required in the other areas and it is hoped that this can be carried out over the next few years. A number of short sections of the Walls are being monitored for structural movement, but it is difficult to anticipate whether major repairs will be necessary. The Walls could be enhanced by further environmental improvements, particularly near the Castle and between the Eastgate and Newgate.

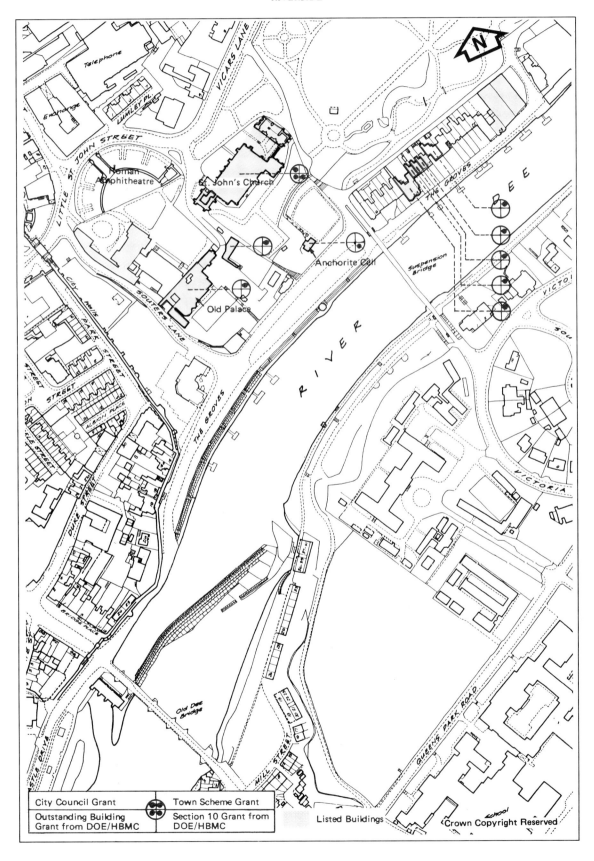

C.8.0
RIVERSIDE

The Riverside is an outstanding recreational amenity for Chester. It is highly popular and well used, with plenty to look at, and good places to walk and sit. The Groves, immediately adjacent to the river, are backed by rising ground, crowned by The Old Palace and St John's Church. The other buildings are of no great distinction but contribute to the pleasant character of the area, with its many small attractive details.

The 1968 Insall Report indicated that the conservation of this area was more a question of protection than action. Few buildings required substantial repair; and only The Old Palace was a matter for anxiety. This fine eighteenth century house, formerly the Bishop's Palace, was occupied by the Y.M.C.A., whose resources were totally inadequate for its proper care. The main problem identified in the report was the conflict between vehicles and pedestrians. During the early 1970s this situation became worse, because the road improvements through Boughton encouraged more motorists to use The Groves to by-pass the city centre. To prevent this, and to reduce traffic in the area, the road adjacent to the Old Dee Bridge was closed in 1970, with a further section behind the bandstand being closed in 1972.

The 1976 Review Study identified major problems with the ruins at the east end of St John's Church, and gave them first priority status. These remains of the former cathedral, dating back to the eleventh century, are an Ancient Monument in the care of the City Council. There was a real danger that part of the masonry would fall onto the footpath below, some of the stones being held in position only by vigorous ivy growth. After extensive discussions with the Department of the Environment, major repairs were started in 1977. This entailed the repair of all dangerous masonry and consolidation of one of the princi-

pal arches that was split face from face. The work was very dangerous, and its successful completion is a tribute to the skill of the masons who carried it out. In 1978, work started on the ruins of the great west tower, which had collapsed in 1881. This necessitated further skilled work to repair the cracked buttresses. Additional repairs were carried out in subsequent years, the work finally being completed in 1981, and the condition of these ruins is now regularly monitored, as structures like this are very susceptible to deterioration.

A local architect was attracted to the Anchorite Cell, a small red sandstone building, dating from the fourteenth century but largely rebuilt in the eighteenth. He obtained a long lease from the Council and restored it for use as his own office; it has since been converted into an unusual home.

In 1978 the Council received an application for a large hotel development at the foot of Souter's Lane immediately below the south-eastern corner of the City Walls. This site was occupied by a bowling green and a group of unsightly corrugated iron sheds. There were a number of individual objections, although some of the amenity societies were generally favourable towards the scheme. The Royal Fine Art Commission, however, believed that the site would be '...a great civic amenity as open space, and that it should

UGLY CORRUGATED IRON BOAT SHEDS AT THE FOOT OF SOUTER'S LANE, NOW REPLACED BY A MODERN RESTAURANT.

THE GROVES BEFORE REPAIRS AND IMPROVEMENTS TOOK PLACE.

not be built on'. Subsequently, the Commission agreed that a restaurant building integrated into a landscape scheme might be acceptable. The Council refused the hotel application, but made it clear that a restaurant or public house would be acceptable in principle. Two further planning applications, with all the attendant discussions and consultations, were approved before the present attractive building was erected.

Towards the end of 1984, the Council became concerned about the extent of alterations which could be carried out to the houses in The Groves without any need for planning approval. The increasing use of long front gardens for car parking was of particular concern. It was recognised that there is little alternative space for parking by the residents, but there was a need to control the extent of any hardstanding, the materials used and the removal of boundary walls. With the approval of the residents, the Council applied to the Department of the Environment for an Article 4 Direction bringing these minor alterations under planning control. This was approved and the Direction issued in June 1985.

As a result of erosion, the river bank along The Groves was slowly collapsing, and it became clear that work would be needed to stabilise the position. Rather than carry out only a minimal repair, the Council decided to take the opportunity to implement substantial improvements.

The first phase of this work, to the east of the suspension bridge, was completed in 1985; involving sheet piling to restrain the river bank, the construction of a two-level promenade and the provision of new seating, lighting and tree planting. Following on from this, the County Council relaid the adjacent roadway with small concrete paviors, the City Council making a contribution towards the additional cost of this material. Further phases of work are planned in the area around the bandstand; and it would be appropriate to consider extending the improvements as far as the Old Dee Bridge.

In 1985 the Y.M.C.A. decided that they could no longer cope with The Old Palace. Work to eliminate dry rot, treat the roof timbers against woodworm and stabilise the foundations of a bay window had been carried out during 1980, but the Association were still unable to maintain the building adequately. At about the same time, British Telecom decided that by 1990 they would be able to vacate the adjacent buildings, which stand over the remains of the Roman Amphitheatre. These decisions, may make it possible to excavate and display the whole of the amphitheatre, together with appropriate interpretative facilities [see E.2.4]. This exciting possibility would provide Chester with another major attraction; the centre-piece of an amenity area that has been protected and enhanced for the benefit of the citizens and their visitors.

VIEW
SOUTH
ACROSS
THE
RING ROAD.

C.9.0
FROM THE NORTHGATE
TO THE BARS

In 1960 the Council adopted a bold traffic plan for the city centre, to solve the inherent problems of twentieth century traffic in an historic city. A new inner ring road was to be constructed around three sides of the compact commercial centre, allied with improvements to the existing roads on the south. Early in 1961, Donald Insall visited the city on behalf of The Georgian Group, to inspect the line of the new road and to discuss alternatives with the City Engineer and Surveyor. It is worth quoting his conclusions at that time:

It is apparent from even a brief visit that much of Chester, within the Walls, calls for redevelopment, and also that if nothing is done to ease the traffic situation, the pressure for alterations at a junction such as that of Watergate Street, Northgate Street, Eastgate Street and Bridge Street, despite the existence of the Rows, could become irresistible. The new road should appreciably reduce this pressure and the new car parks would allow the banning of roadside parking in the busier streets. Any alterations would either involve the destruction of a large number of important buildings and pleasant streets, or would be so far from the centre that they would not be effective in reducing the congestion.

The new road claimed few notable victims apart from Egerton House, a fine eighteenth century building, listed Grade I, which stood on the site of the Northgate roundabout. Nevertheless, areas of small scale nineteenth century development to the north and east of the centre were badly affected. By the time of the 1968 Insall Report construction work was in progress, and it was apparent that however beneficial the new road might be, its effect on the fabric of the city would be traumatic. The report comments:

Road design and construction is one of the country's biggest investments. Yet unlike individual buildings, which fall within detailed town planning control, urban roads receive little co-ordinated environmental design.

The inner ring road has brought major changes to the north-east section of the city centre. The 1964 Grenfell Baines Plan recommended that virtually the whole of the Gorse Stacks and Canalside area should be redeveloped. The 1968 Insall report agreed with this proposal, particularly with regard to the area north of Foregate Street. The character of the area had little to recommend it, with much dereliction and small groups of once attractive buildings marooned in a sea of cleared sites, temporary car parks and

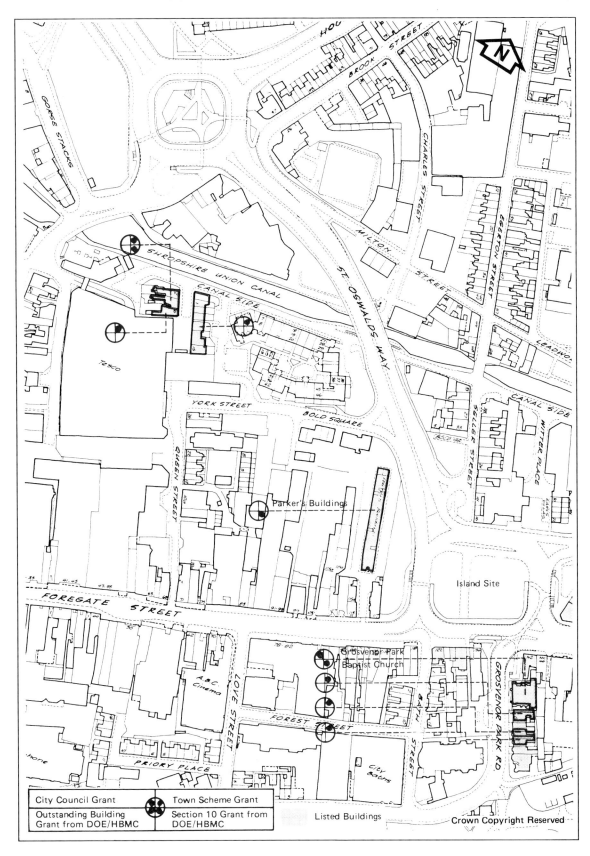

| City Council Grant | | Town Scheme Grant |
| Outstanding Building Grant from DOE/HBMC | | Section 10 Grant from DOE/HBMC |

Listed Buildings

Crown Copyright Reserved

makeshift premises.

In 1972 discussions started on preliminary proposals for development immediately south of the canal. This involved a hotel north of the Kaleyards and a commercial development between Frodsham Street and Queen Street, comprising 150,000 square feet of shopping space, with parking for 1,200 cars, together with housing to the east of Queen Street. At the same time proposals for 77,000 square feet of shopping with 450 car parking spaces on the site of Parker's Buildings were also being discussed [see C.9.2].

The Council were concerned at the scale of these proposals and appointed a specialist economic counsultant who indicated that, with a growth in population, together with increasing tourist spending, Chester could support a further 125,000 square feet of shopping space up to 1981. The consultant advised that in the interest of maintaining a compact shopping centre, the development adjacent to Frodsham Street was preferable to the Parker's Buildings proposal.

In 1973 a much larger scheme was submitted for outline approval. This consisted of a 200 bedroom hotel and conference centre on Gorse Stacks, with development east of Frodsham Street providing 200,000 square feet of shopping, 200,000 square feet of offices, 1,200 car parking spaces, and a small number of flats. Discussions continued over the next two years before an outline approval was given, the Council being concerned to reduce the areas of shopping and office space, to increase the residential content of the scheme and to retain the eighteenth century houses at the north end of Queen Street. A Housing Association promoted the development of flats and maisonettes adjacent to the ring road and the restoration and refurbishment of the eighteenth century houses in what became Queens Place. This has provided the core of a revitalised residential area close to the city centre.

During the first half of 1976, problems with financial backing for the scheme led to a change of developer. New discussions were held on a reduced com-

mercial scheme, omitting the hotel and conference centre, but the Council were again concerned at the scale of the proposals and at one point it was noted that:

...the proposals could not be recommended for acceptance. Though time might not be on the side of the interested parties, it was on the side of the City, in the sense that the City could, if necessary, live with this run-down area for the next ten years, but if the Council was rushed into approval of a scheme which fell short of what is good for the City, the City would have many years to repent it.

An outline scheme was eventually approved, but when the detailed design was well advanced the owners of a key strip of land across the centre of the site changed their minds and decided not to sell. This necessitated a rapid rethink; the development was split, with one section fronting Foregate Street and the other Frodsham Street. The Council considered that this enforced reduction in the size of the scheme was, if anything, an improvement; and because of the developer's tight timetable gave informal approval so that detailed design work could start immediately. Construction work started in 1978 and was completed in November 1980. At the suggestion of the Conservation Area Advisory Committee the final scheme incorporated the rebuilt facades of the Queen Street Congregation Church, which had been previously vandalised, damaged by fire and gutted, as focal points at the rear of the development.

A letter to the Chester Observer by Gilbert H. Parry, Chairman of the Conservation Area Advisory Committee in December 1980 made the following comments on the development:

But buildings don't just happen.
The preliminary works on this development...
entailed a tremendous amount of hard work,
and tenacious negotiating...
...those who have had the tenacity to steer it through and those who have been concerned with trying to fit in the new architecture...can now rest in the knowledge that they were right.

The Conservation Area Advisory

Committee was also closely involved in a proposal for development of a site at the top of Frodsham Street, adjacent to the canal. The original scheme was for a three storey building. The Committee raised substantial objections because this would adversely affect important views of the cathedral from the north-west side of the city. Following discussions, the proposed height of the majority of the building was reduced, leaving only a tower to rise above two storeys, as a focal point to the corner.

Despite all this new development, which includes some new Council housing to the north of Parker's Buildings, the surroundings of the ring road still look incomplete and untidy. The proposed hotel on Gorse Stakes has not been implemented; the Rank Bingo Club looks like a stranded whale, having no relationship with its surroundings; the back ends of buildings in Delamere Street and George Street are as unsightly as ever; the Island site remains empty; and the scarred ends of buildings in Foregate Street remain unhealed. Planting a few trees will not hide these environmental problems. Further new development such as proposed in the 1968 Insall Report for the Northgate roundabout, appears to be the only way the area can be improved.

C.9.1

GROSVENOR PARK BAPTIST CHURCH
Faith, Hope and Charity.

The Baptist Church was designed in 1879 by John Douglas, together with the adjacent terrace of six houses. Although the houses vary in design, the whole group, including the church, is built in the same Ruabon brick and forms an important architectural composition, which is listed Grade II.

During 1974 the architects acting for the church obtained a specialist report on the building. This indicated that as a result of missing roof tiles, blocked rainwater goods and bad pointing, there were outbreaks of wet and dry rot in the main roof and one of the turret roofs, behind the dado panelling and in the floor of the church, vestibule and vestries. Even with grant aid, the congregation were not able

to consider spending the £30,000 necessary to put the building into a reasonable state of repair. An application for listed building consent to demolish the church was submitted in May 1977. There were objections to this proposal from the Chester Civic Trust, the Victorian Society, the Ancient Monuments Society, the City's Conservation Area Advisory Committee and a number of local people; and the Council refused the application.

During the next two years, no progress was made in finding a solution, and the church authorities decided to try and sell the building. This proved unsuccessful; and in March 1980 a further application was made to demolish it. This was again refused.

Almost immediately the Society of St Vincent de Paul expressed interest in acquiring the church, as a night shelter for the homeless. They proposed initially to use the basement accommodation, and in the long term to extend into the church itself, probably erecting a mezzanine floor to take advantage of the height of the space. Despite objections from local residents, this proposal was supported by the Council.

Then quite unexpectedly, while the Society of St Vincent de Paul were finalising their offer for the building, the church authorities decided to sell to a couple who wished to start a 'fundamental Protestant' congregation in Chester. In an article in a local paper it was suggested that the building was really too big for them and the couple are quoted as saying:
...we haven't two pennies to rub together.
and:

I know the church needs a lot of repairs although we have not had an independent survey. We must just pray to God and he will provide. If the money comes we will do the repairs and if it doesn't we won't.

As a result of this situation the Council had urgent discussions with the new owners, both to advise them about the condition of the building and to clarify their intentions. The owners agreed to commission a report on the condition of the building, but it soon became clear that they did not have the resources to pay an architect.

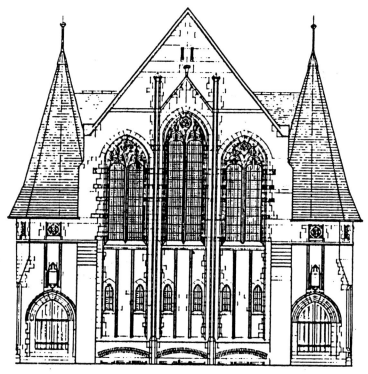

GROSVENOR PARK BAPTIST CHURCH.

The Council therefore decided to appoint one themselves, so that the full extent of the repairs could be determined. During this period, the Department of the Environment was refusing to consider Section 10 grant applications; but in view of the urgency the Council went ahead with the appointment, on the basis that this would not prejudice a retrospective application. When the application was submitted the Historic Buildings Council felt unable to recommend to the Department that a grant be offered because:

...the study appears to have been carried out as a theoretical exercise to establish the extent of the repairs and remedial action necessary, rather than as a preliminary to positive action to secure the restoration of the building. While it remains in its present ownership there is apparently little hope of the recommended work being carried out voluntarily and there is no mention of a Repairs Notice.

However after a further request from the Council, indicating that the study was an important preliminary stage to the eventual repair of the building, the Department of the Environment did make a grant towards the cost of the architect's fees.

The report indicated that urgent works costing approximately £40,000 were required, of which £18,000 was concerned with the elimination of dry rot. The owners said that they were willing to start repair work; and the Council offered a 25% grant towards the dry rot eradication as a first phase. A matching Section 10 grant was offered by the Department of the Environment.

Despite these grants, the work did not start, because the owners could not raise the balance of the costs. The City Council was unable to take any legal action in the form of a Repairs Notice and compulsory purchase, because Section 115 of the Town and Country Planning Act 1971 does not apply to 'buildings in ecclesiastical use'. After a year of little activity, a meeting was held in March 1983 to see on what basis there might be progress. This established that the congregation of 12-20 people would probably be able to raise or borrow about £12,000 towards repair costs, now estimated at £60,000. It was also agreed that there was little point in carrying out the first phase of works to eliminate the dry rot, unless this could be closely followed by a second phase to prevent further deterioration.

The Council tried to persuade the owners to sell the church, but they were not prepared to consider this option. The only other courses open to the Council were to substantially increase the level of grant aid, or to await the demolition of the building.

In July 1983 the Council offered a 40% grant, which was matched by a Section 10 grant from the Department of the Environment. In view of these high percentages the grants were tied to legal agreements which extended the grant reclaim period to 10 years in the event of the building being sold, and ensured that ownership would transfer to the Council if the repair was not completed.

The Council were also concerned to guarantee that the church had sufficient funds available for their contribution, and that they would be reserved specifically for the repair scheme. It therefore approved a loan of £6,000 to make up any shortfall in the Church resources, and also agreed to act as the church's agent for the purpose of paying the contractor and obtaining the grants. This ensured that the church's contribution to the scheme was deposited with the Council before the contract for the work was signed and public money committed.

Work started on site in October 1984 and was largely completed by the end of 1985. The complex payment arrangements created problems when costs rose as a result of the discovery of further outbreaks of dry rot. At one time there were insufficient funds to pay the contractor, and he threatened to withdraw from site. This problem was resolved; but as the repairs neared completion, the architect halted work so that the financial position could be assessed. Fortunately the church were able to make further funds available and the grants were accordingly increased to cover the additional costs.

As a result of the willingness of both the Council and the Department of the Environment to provide very high percentages of grant, this important church has been saved.

———

C.9.2
PARKERS' BUILDINGS
Keeping Victorian Cottage Flats

Parker's Buildings lie on the north side of Foregate Street, immediately adjacent to the inner ring road. They were built in 1888-89 to designs by the noted Chester architects, Douglas and Fordham, as part of a

redevelopment by the 1st Duke of Westminster, reflecting his interest as a patron of the Improved Industrial Dwellings Company. The development included business premises facing onto Foregate Street, flanking a forecourt which provides access to Parker's Buildings. The buildings on the frontage were designed in Douglas' loose interpretation of an early seventeenth century style, with a rich vocabulary of detail, including diapered brickwork, shaped gables and bold chimneys. Parker's Buildings themselves consisted of thirty cottage flats, arranged as a three storey block with access from open stairways and balconies, and built in a simplified version of the style.

In the early 1970s the City Council were conscious that there was a need for additional car parking on the eastern side of the city centre; and identified the site of Parker's Buildings as suitable for a multistorey car park. After discussions with a number of developers, outline planning approval was granted in 1975 for a proposal incorporating shops, offices, an entertainment area and a car park. The consent stipulated that the Douglas buildings fronting Foregate Street would have to be substantially retained, and that no demolition should take place in advance of a firm contract to proceed with the new development.

This consent was not implemented; but over the next few years a number of proposals were received from different developers interested in various commercial possibilities. During this period the Council's policies changed, and the draft Local Plan stressed the important of maintaining and replacing residential accommodation in the City Centre. The Plan also specifically identified Parker's Buildings as being suitable for rehabilitation.

During 1978 the owners were again negotiating for commercial development of the site; but they agreed to sell it to the Council, at a price which reflected the site's commercial potential. The purchase was agreed, subject to a grant from the Department of the Environment, calculated to offset the difference between the commercial

value of the site and the residential value of the buildings. This was forthcoming; the purchase was completed in February 1979 and the property sold on to a Housing Association in the following month.

In October 1979 the Council asked the Department of the Environment to spot-list Parker's Buildings and the two associated buildings fronting Foregate Street. Despite the support of the Victorian Society and the Royal Fine Art Commission, this request was refused on the basis that:

We do not regard the fact that they are 'industrial' dwellings important enough to justify listing on historical grounds while the architectural features, though pleasing and mildly original, are not distinctive enough for buildings of such a late date.

The design of the scheme for modernisation was generally developing well, but there were some differences of opinion between the Council and the Department of the Environment on one side and the Housing Association on the other, over what constituted appropriate alterations. The main

balconies, which the Association wished to problems revolved around the staircase enclose, and the design of a satisfactory replacement window. The window design was finally resolved, and the open balconies were retained despite the Association's view that they added to the regimented workhouse image. Work started on site in June 1980 and was completed eighteen months later, the restoration works receiving a Section 10 grant from the Department of the Environment. As a result, a fine building has been preserved and the residential capacity of the city centre improved.

C.10.0
TOWARDS THE STATION

In April 1980 the Council designated a small conservation area covering the main frontage of the station and other nineteenth century buildings around the forecourt. Soon afterwards, the City Centre Conservation Area was extended to include Egerton Street, an area of interesting early nineteenth century housing.

A DERELICT CANALSIDE HOUSE IN EGERTON STREET.

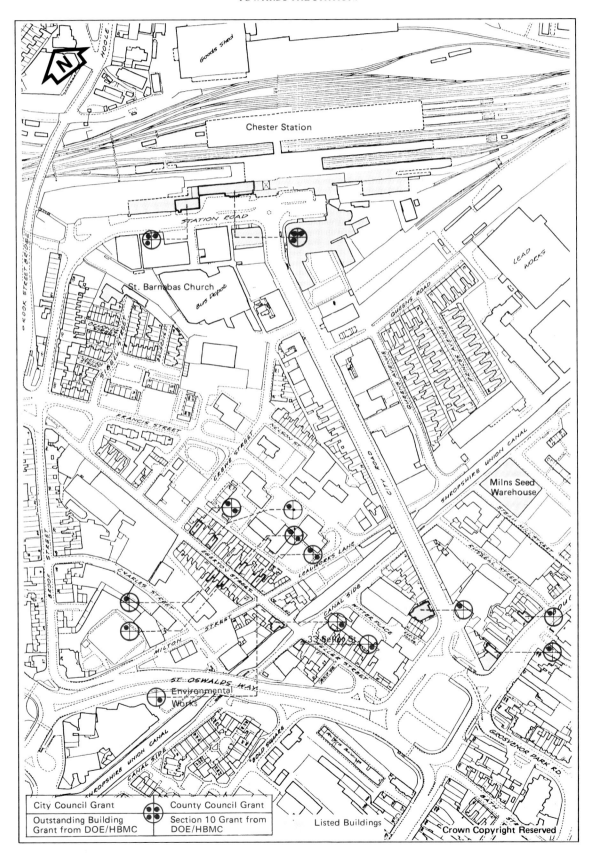

Chester Station

St. Barnabas Church

Milns Seed Warehouse

LEAD WORKS

City Council Grant	County Council Grant
Outstanding Building Grant from DOE/HBMC	Section 10 Grant from DOE/HBMC

Listed Buildings

Crown Copyright Reserved

Over the next four years, the Council investigated ways of restoring and improving the houses in Egerton Street. Initially two key blocks of buildings were proposed for Section 10 grants, but these were refused by the Department of the Environment. Then a Housing Action Area was declared, but this could not guarantee the conservation of the area's character. An Article Four Direction was approved so as to provide some addition planning control, but that did not encourage repairs. An 'enveloping' scheme, with all external repairs being carried out by the Council under a single contract, was next investigated, but this could not obtain the necessary approvals. Finally a Section 10 scheme was proposed, similar to the one operating in Albion Street [see C.6.0].

In September 1984 the future of the Section 10 grant programme was discussed at a meeting with the Historic Buildings and Monuments Commission, with particular reference to Egerton Street. The Commission agreed that the programme could be extended to include Egerton Street if the City Council took a comprehensive view of the area, including the approaches from the station. As a result, the City Centre Conservation Area was again extended, absorbing the Chester Station Conservation Area and including City Road, Brook Street and an important stretch of the canal.

The Egerton Street scheme was then initiated and has had some success. However, the long delay in finding a satisfactory arrangement damaged the area by creating frustration and disillusionment among the residents. Some buildings were unsympathetically 'improved', while others deteriorated to the point where partial demolition was necessary.

The buildings on the east side of Seller Street have concerned the Council for many years. They were small nineteenth century houses with some good details, but the majority are empty and rapidly deteriorating. After discussions with the various owners, a planning appraisal of the area was approved in May 1984. It was hoped that this would generate sufficient sense of certainty in the future of the street to encourage repairs.

This has not proved to be the case; and negotiations with the owner of the majority of the buildings have been delayed by complications in the sale of the former Post Office by the Council. Although the Historic Buildings and Monuments Commission generally considered these buildings to be of insufficient importance or priority to justify a Section 10 grant, the restoration of No 33 Seller Street has received a grant because of its relationship to Egerton Street. This may be the first glimmer of hope for the street.

In March 1985 the Council considered the conservation problems of Brook Street. This street contains a number of Victorian shopfronts, but there was pressure for their renewal with modern materials or replacement with solid brick, rendered or stone-clad facades. These changes were eroding the character of the street and reducing its appeal to shoppers. The Council decided to resist applications for alterations to the good Victorian facades and to offer grant aid for their restoration.

The future character of this area is still in doubt. It is unlikely that all the Egerton Street properties will have been repaired before the end of the scheme in 1987; none of the Brook Street traders have shown any interest in the offer of grant aid; the Seller Street houses continue to rot; and St Barnabas' Church, Sibell Street, is on the market, with a roof that needs urgent attention. However there are also signs of progress. The Conservation Area Advisory Committee is promoting environmental improvements for City Road; the intensive use of the Milns Seeds Warehouse may stimulate further improvements along the canal; and the Visitors in Chester Study recognised the importance of the area, as the railway traveller's first impression of the city.

———

C.10.1

CHESTER STATION
"We're getting there"

The station is a large Italianate building designed by Francis Thompson, in conjunction with Robert Stephenson and C H Wild. The central block was built in 1847-48, and it was later extended in the same

of the most splendid early railway stations, extremely long...'

In October 1967 the British Railways Board applied for permission to demolish the Mold Wing, at the western end of the station, together with the adjoining arcaded shed. The building was in a poor condition and had extensive dry rot. The Improvement Committee of the Council decided not to oppose the demolition of the Mold Wing, but the matter was deferred so that the views of the Minister of Housing and Local Government could be obtained. In May, the Minister decided that he would not be justified in insisting on the retention of the Mold Wing. By this time the Improvement Committee appeared to be having second thoughts, and made a series of requests for further information on the proposed appearance of the site following demolition. During September and October a number of objections to the demolition were received, in particular from the Victorian Society and the Chester Civic Trust; and the Council finally decided to refuse the application. The Board appealed, but following a public enquiry the Council's view was upheld.

Following this refusal, the Railways Board made some efforts to find suitable tenants for the Mold Wing, but the cost of restoration was prohibitive. In 1977 an ambitious modernisation of the whole station complex was proposed; but following a report from consultants, certain sections of the building were identified as unsafe. Work to eliminate dry rot and renovate the West Wing was undertaken at a cost of £75,000, during which a builder fell through a floor. However the cost of putting the whole building into a good state of repair was considered to be too high. At this stage British Rail indicated that the majority of the building was surplus to their requirement, but there was little interest from possible tenants.

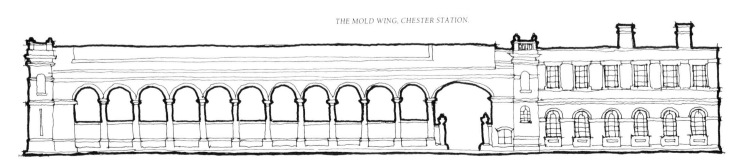

Then in 1979 a fire gutted the Mold Wing. This acted as a stimulus; and a local firm of architects opened negotiations to acquire this section of the building from British Rail. Their scheme for the building was dependant upon the level of grant aid available for the restoration of the exterior. After protracted negotiations, grant applications were submitted to the Department of the Environment, the County Council and the City Council. The City Council designated the Chester Station Conservation Area and agreed to a substantial grant, the Department of the Environment upgraded the buildings to Grade II* and offered a Section 4 grant, and the County Council offered a further small grant. All this

INTERIOR OF THE MOLD WING FOLLOWING THE FIRE OF 1979.

enabled work to start on site in November 1981.

Despite the restoration of the Mold Wing, the bulk of the station building was still a problem. At a meeting between British Rail and the Council in June 1981, it was agreed that the main problems were the sheer size of the building, its excess of accommodation and the cost of repair work. The matter was further complicated by British Rail's continuing uncertainty about its own requirements. As a result of this meeting the Council resolved to take legal action and to note the financial implications of any grant applications that might be received from potential lessees.

By early 1982 it was clear that a local developer was seriously interested and legal action was therefore postponed. A grant application was made to the Department of the Environment, who had indicated that they would expect British Rail to dispose of the building at a 'nil value' and to make a contribution towards the costs of repair. With repair costs estimated at £650,000 it was tentatively proposed that half this cost might be met by equal contributions from the Department of the Environment, the City Council and British Rail. This would have amounted to over £20,000 from each body in every year during a five year period. This was at a time when the Council were only able to allocate £5,000 per annum for grants to buildings in the urban area of the district. Despite this financial implication, the Council restated its commitment to the restoration of the station. Unfortunately, by the middle of 1982, the local developer had decided to back out of the proposal.

Almost immediately the company who had restored the Mold Wing expressed an interest in acquiring the West Wing. After extensive discussions, a price of £1 was agreed with British Rail and grants were offered by the Department of the Environment, the County Council and the City Council. Work started on site in January 1985 and was completed within eight months.

Despite the successful restoration of half of the station building the East Wing is still a matter of concern. British Rail remain undecided about their requirements; and the building is deteriorating.

C.11.0

OUTSIDE THE CITY CENTRE

In the early 1970s the Council made a number of small grants to buildings outside the city centre, but conservation interest in the urban and rural areas really began with the preparation of the 1976 Review Studies. These recognised the visual importance of certain areas and their vulnerability to change.

During the preparation of the Urban Area Study the Council became aware of development proposals that would involve the demolition of three nineteenth century houses in Flookersbrook, a small residential area of considerable character to the north-east of the city centre. Discussions with the Department of the

REDCLIFFE, QUEEN'S PARK, A LARGE VICTORIAN VILLA, NOW SUCCESSFULLY SUB-DIVIDED INTO SMALLER RESIDENTIAL UNITS.

August 1976. The Council then designated the Flookersbrook Conservation Area, producing a planning brief that outlined acceptable development.

In addition to the Flookersbrook Conservation Area, the 1976 Review Study recommended that the predominantly nineteenth century suburbs to the east and south of the city centre should become conservation areas. After extensive local consultation, this proposal was implemented during 1979 with the desig-

ATTRACTIVE VICTORIAN HOUSES IN THE QUEEN'S PARK CONSERVATION AREA.

nation of four areas; Boughton and the Meadows, Queens Park, Handbridge and Curzon Park. At the same time a specific urban area budget was established within the Conservation Fund.

At Local Government reorganisation in 1974 the new City Council took responsibility for a large rural area, including sixteen conservation areas. As a result of the Rural Area Study more conservation areas were designated [see G.2] and additional finance for grants to rural buildings was gradually made available.

The diversity of the character and problems of the urban and rural areas makes it almost impossible to summarise the Council's policy, but every opportunity has been taken to conserve and enhance. The County Council were encouraged to provide appropriate walls and railings along the road widening in Boughton. A Job Creation Scheme for the improvement of the woodland area of Flookersbrook was jointly funded by the residents, the City and County Councils and the Civic Trust. A planning brief for the development of land in Queen's Park was produced, ensuring that the mature

BOUGHTON RIVERSIDE.

trees and earth mounding, characteristic of the area, would be respected and retained. The restoration of many individual buildings has been grant aided. And so the work goes on!

In 1984 the Council and the Historic Buildings and Monuments Commission instituted a special grant scheme for Boughton Riverside. This area of the Boughton and Meadows Conservation Area is a steep escarpment, above a bend in the river. It was developed during the eighteenth and nineteenth centuries with a variety of buildings of great townscape value. The view when walking along the Meadows or travelling down the river is of a continually changing silhouette, produced by a varied roofscape of chimneys, turrets and spires. The mixture of architectural styles, together with the variety of individual materials and details, add up to a complex but satisfying whole. The character of the area relies upon the many small ancillary structures and the decorative features on the houses. Many of these elements are beginning to deteriorate, repair costs are substantial and they are not necessary to the owners of the properties. The grant scheme is designed to encourage restoration of these features on buildings otherwise in sound condition, with Section 10 grants from the Commission matched by grants from the Council. Also an Article 4 Direction has been approved, to give additional planning control over these minor, but important, details.

Over the next few years the main concern in the suburban conservation areas will be how to control the continuing changes in their historic character. There is constant pressure. Changing uses for the larger houses creates problems of additional car parking, sub-division of gardens and alterations to the buildings. Proposals to insert new houses into gardens and other open spaces could seriously affect the balance between buildings and landscape. The wish to 'modernise' often leads to the loss of historic details on many minor, but visually important, buildings. Further policies to control these changes are required, to maintain the fine character of the city's suburbs.

CHURCH BANK TATTENHALL,
EARLY NINETEENTH CENTURY COTTAGES CONTRIBUTE TO THE
CHARACTER OF THE CONSERVATION AREA.

The rural conservation areas are generally under less pressure for change and the primary concern will be to prevent the steady erosion of character resulting from the use of standard details in new buildings and modernisations. This needs to be complemented by a policy of small scale enhancement projects.

C.11.1
GREENBANK EATON ROAD
A Problem Bequest.

Greenbank is a large Regency house of 1820 on the south side of the city, listed Grade II. In 1923 Peter Jones, a local industrialist, commissioned Sir Charles Reilly to carry out alterations, probably including the erection of the fine neo-classical gatehouse. Jones was a friend and patron of C. R. Ashbee, a leading figure of the Arts and Crafts Movement, who designed some furniture for the house. Unfortunately, later in life he removed the principal staircase and other internal features.

The house, together with eleven acres of land was bequeathed in trust to the City of Chester by Peter Jones in 1960, for the '...purpose of adult education, the training of teachers, or for the training of young persons in good citizenship'. The City Council formally accepted the property in January 1962, but almost immediately there were doubts as to whether the City could afford to repair and maintain the house. In April 1962 the Finance Committee heard that immediate repairs would cost £3,500; and in July a proposal to rescind acceptance of the property was only lost on the Mayor's casting vote.

Between 1962 and 1968 the Education Committee tried to find some way of using Greenbank consistent with the terms of the trust; but the estimated cost of restoration and adaptations, plus the annual running costs, were prohibitive. As trustees, the Education Committee had power of sale, provided the proceeds were used to fulfil the original intentions of the donor. The Department of Education and Science confirmed this power of sale, and an independent surveyor's report was commissioned. This report emphasised the high value of the land and indicated that the demolition of the house would enable the most advantageous price to be obtained.

During 1969 two developers showed interest in the site for housing and an outline planning approval was granted. The Council now found themselves in a dilemma. The house had only been in occasional use for the past ten years and was deteriorating rapidly. As Trustees of the Peter Jones Foundation, they were under an obligation to obtain the best possible price for the property; and this would involve the demolition of the house. Yet they would find it extremely embarrassing to apply for permission to demolish this listed building, at a time when they were encouraging owners of similar buildings to preserve them.

To resolve the matter, the Council decided to test whether permission could be obtained for the demolition of the house; and an application for listed building consent was submitted in May 1971. There were substantial objections to this proposal from the Chester Civic Trust, the Chester Archaeological Society, The Georgian Group and the Victorian Society. The Department

GREENBANK, EATON ROAD.

of the Environment accordingly decided that a public inquiry should be held. To avoid this situation the Council withdrew the application and decided to look for alternative proposals that would retain the house.

In October 1972 the City Council accepted a suggestion from the Department of Education and Science that Cheshire County Council be asked to assume trusteeship of the Peter Jones Foundation, as part of Local Government Reorganisation. This proposal was accepted by both Councils, and Greenbank was transferred in 1973. At the same time the City Council informed the County Council that they would object to any plans to sell the associated land for private housing development.

Between 1974 and 1976, the County Council spent some £12,000 on emergency repair work while the future of the property was considered. There seemed little prospect of the house being suitable for any educational use, and in April 1977 permission was granted for change of use to offices, together with an outline approval for 5,000 square feet of new offices to be built in the grounds. This scheme failed because of the high cost of restoring the house, and an application was submitted for residential development of the land. This was refused by the City Council on the grounds that there was no requirement to release land in this area for housing; but a similar application in the following year was approved, on the understanding that the proceeds of the sale of the land would be put towards the renovation of the house.

The County Council explored various alternative uses for the building; eventually deciding to convert it into a trainee catering establishment in connection with the Chester College of Further Education. Restoration work started in 1980; but by that time the building was in a very poor state. The loss of many historic features, including a verandah and conservatory on the garden elevations, had to be accepted, but the appearance of the building from Eaton Road has been retained. After twenty years of deterioration and all the attendant problems, Greenbank now fulfils the terms of the bequest.

C.11.2

SHOTWICK VILLAGE
Conserving an Estate Village

Shotwick lies five miles north-west of Chester on the edge of the Wirral Peninsula. It is one of the few surviving manorial settlements in the County, having both its manor house and the majority of the land still in a single ownership. Its present seclusion, at the end of a narrow road, belies its medieval importance; when the ford across the Dee and the associated quay were protected by a castle, and the village was at the hub of communications for both trade and military activity. The layout of the village has remained largely unaltered since the seventeenth century, when the silting up of the river led to a decline in prosperity, and the majority of the buildings date from the seventeenth or early eighteenth centuries. The Shotwick Conservation Area was designated by the County Council in February 1974, just before Local Government Reorganisation.

Initially, there was disagreement between the owner of the estate and his agent on the one side, and the City Council on the other. This revolved around two problems, Firstly, the owner wished to erect one or two new houses in the village, largely in order to increase the estate income so that the historic buildings could be restored and improved. This idea was resisted by both the City and County Councils, because it was contary to their policies and would change the whole character of the village. Secondly, the extensive restoration of Shotwick Hall which was carried out in phases between 1974 and 1977, received grants from the Department of the Environment, the County Council and the former Chester Rural District Council, but the new City Council were unable to offer a grant because of other conservation commitments.

Matters were not improved by the publication of the 1976 Review Study which reported that virtually all the buildings in the village required some repairs and identified five that needed urgent attention. The study also stated that the Shotwick Conservation Area was:

...one of the worst in terms of condition of buildings and whilst not denigrating the activities of the estate owner, the situation of disrepair has been continuing for some time. Of all the conservation areas studied Shotwick needs an urgent and considerable injection of finance from all sources if the buildings and character are to be maintained.

The owner was angered by the apparent lack of recognition of all that had been done in Shotwick over the previous decade:

When I inherited Shotwick in 1964 it was in a pitiful run-down state, mortgaged and yielding uneconomic rents. In addition to having to foot a heavy death duty bill, I had to set about modernising all the cottages, as well as carry out essential but long outstanding expensive repairs. The work of 'modernisation' is now nearly completed, but I am the first to realise that the work of restoration has really only just begun.

The Review Study recommended that priority should be given to grant aiding the restoration of the estate farms and cottages. This led to grants from the City Council, County Council and Civic Trust for the restoration of Church Cottage in 1978-79. It was, however, clear that if a programme of restoration were to be attempted, greater financial assistance would be required. Therefore, in 1980 the City Council applied to the Department of the Environment for the conservation area to be accepted as 'outstanding' so that Section 10 grants could be made available. This was linked to an application for grant towards the comprehensive restoration of Greyhound Farm.

'Outstanding' status was agreed in October 1980, but the grant application for Greyhound Farm was deferred because of a lack of funds for grants. Nevertheless, work started on site, incorporating a number of additional items requested by the Department's architect. Unfortunately, owing to a number of misunderstandings and confusion over the inspection of the work, the work did not meet the standards of either the Department or the Council. In particular the window details were found to be incorrect and the repointing was very poor. After much discussion and argument the Council paid their grant, but substantial pressure had to be applied by the agent before the Department eventually agreed to pay grant for those items which had been satisfactorily completed.

By this time the basis for Section 10 grants had been revised and it became necessary for the Estate to submit a programme of repairs for approval. The unfortunate experience at Greyhound Farm had

SHOTWICK VILLAGE.

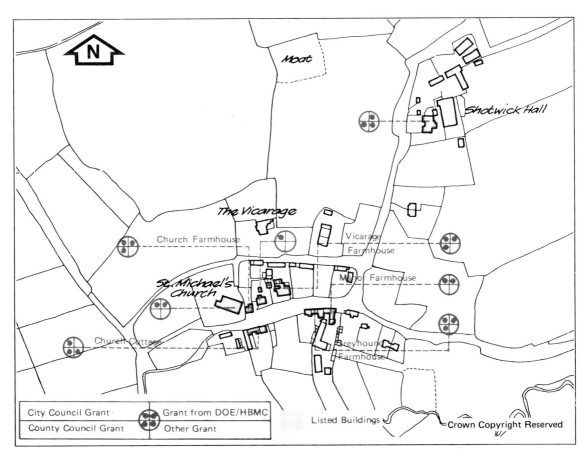

CAST IRON 'GOTHICK' WINDOW
AT MANOR FARM, SHOTWICK.

altered the Department's attitude toward Shotwick and there seemed little prospect of obtaining further grants. However, the City Council continued to press the case, stressing the historic value of the village and its buildings and the urgent need for financial assistance. By the end of 1981 it was agreed that a Section 10 programme should be submitted; and this was prepared, together with an application for assistance towards the restoration of Manor Farm.

A section 10 grant for Manor Farm was offered in March 1983 on the basis of the submitted programme. Since then the restoration programme has proceeded reasonably smoothly; the Council matching the Section 10 grants and with some additional financial support from the County Council. Work on Manor Farm was completed in June 1983, a comprehensive scheme on Vicarage Farm was carried out during 1985 and discussions are in progress about Church House Farm. None of this work is

really economic for the estate owner. Even with the benefit of grants, he has had to spend more than is justified by the rentals received.

The programme of restoration will need to continue for some time yet. Further work is required on some of the houses, where only holding repairs have been possible in the past, and many of the outbuildings which make up the character of the village require substantial attention. Nevertheless, the owner of Shotwick can now be proud of what has been achieved; the historic houses of the village have been improved and re- stored, yet the secluded character of the place remains unspoilt.

———

C.11.3
ROCK FARM, ELTON
Scrapyard, Power Station and
Historic Building

Elton was once a small agricultural village on the edge of the marshland along the estuary of the River Mersey. The historic core is now swamped by a large and depressingly standardised housing estate on one side and by major industrial development, including the Ince Power Station, on the other. Rock Farm, listed Grade II*, is the most significant building within the Elton Conservation Area. The brick front dates from the eighteenth century, but conceals an early timber framed structure that was significantly altered in 1626.

Immediately after the designation of the conservation area in 1979, the Council assessed the condition of the buildings within the area, decided that Rock Farm required urgent work and appointed a consultant architect to report on the building and suggest future uses. This report was completed in June 1980 and indicated that the structure was in poor condition and that some of the ornamental plaster in the interior had already collapsed. The land at the rear was occupied by a haulage contractor and there was a scrapyard immediately adjacent.

As the owner was elderly and in very poor health the Council delayed taking any legal action, although there was regular correspondence with her agents. On her death in 1981, the haulage company indicated that it was willing to move, provided an alternative site could be found; and the principle of the Council's acquisition was agreed. Finalising the details of the proposal took over three years. In 1982 an alternative site for the haulage company was refused planning permission by an adjacent planning authority, and in the following year the Council served a Repairs Notice with the intention of stimulating the negotiations.

In February 1984 the Council granted planning permission for the relocation of the haulage company onto a local industrial estate; and the purchase of Rock Farm was completed in March 1985 with the assistance of an acquisition grant from the Department of the Environment. In the meantime the consultant architect had carried out a further survey and recommended emergency shoring to prevent a collapse of the front gables. This work was carried out, together with other urgent works to secure the building.

While the negotiations over the purchase had been proceeding, the structure had deteriorated significantly; and it was decided that the building was unlikely to survive further delay until it could be sold to someone prepared to carry out the restoration. The Council therefore proceeded to carry out repairs to the structural shell, leaving internal repairs and improvements for a new owner. A grant towards the cost of this work was sought from the Historic Buildings and Monuments Commission, initially on the basis that the house was of outstanding architectural or historic interest. This failed. The Council then sought to promote a Section 10 grant for the Elton Conservation Area, believing that the restoration of Rock Farm would act as a catalyst for other improvements in the area. This also failed, but following further investigations a grant was given, since a Repairs Notice had been used to secure the preservation of the building.

The main structural restoration, including the reinstatement of the ornamental plaster ceiling, was completed in April 1986. Rock Farm was advertised for sale, with a stipulation that the new owner would carry out the necessary internal repairs. Probably as a result of the location of the building, adjacent to a scrapyard and with a fine view of the power station, only one offer was received. Nevertheless, this historic farmhouse has been saved, and will undoubtedly stimulate further improvements to the Elton Conservation Area.

ROCK FARM, ELTON.

THE BEAR AND BILLET, LOWER BRIDGE STREET.

D

ACHIEVEMENTS, FAILURES AND PROBLEMS

These ancient dwellings present every shade and degree of historical colour and

expression. Some are dark with neglect and deformity....

Others stand there square-shouldered and sturdy, with their beams painted and

straightened, their plaster whitewashed, their carvings polished....

It is noticeable that the actual townfolk have bravely accepted the situation bequeathed

by the past, and the large number of rich and intelligent restorations

of the old facades marks an effective jumble of their piety and their policy.

These elaborate and ingenious repairs attest a highly informed consciousness of

the pictorial value of the city....

Henry James,
The Nation,
1872

ACHIEVEMENTS, FAILURES AND PROBLEMS

THE CHESTER Conservation Programme is an acknowledged success. In 1981 the City received the European Prize for the Preservation of Historic Monuments, awarded by the FVS Foundation of Hamburg. The Council's work in the Bridgegate Action Area was recognised in 1983 by the presentation of a Europa Nostra Medal and the Conservation Programme was highly commended by the Royal Town Planning Institute in 1985. Numerous individual projects have also received awards.

The City is regularly visited by professionals from many countries who wish to know how Chester has approached the problems of revitalising a historic environment. This is in addition to the many general interest groups and the visits from schools and colleges, all of whom wish to see what the City has achieved.

In this section the Conservation Programme is examined in a spirit of self criticism to identify its achievements, its failures and the continuing problems. Conservation is not finite, with a fixed end date or goal. It has to respond to a constantly changing situation and many matters have to be classified as continuing concerns rather than achievements or failures.

D.1.0
ACHIEVEMENTS

It is easy to say that the Conservation Programme has been a 'success', but it is now very difficult to remember what the centre of Chester was like twenty years ago, and to appreciate the scale of the achievement. This section attempts to analyse the 'success', breaking it down into different areas of activity.

THE EUROPEAN PRIZE
FOR THE PRESERVATION
OF HISTORIC MONUMENTS.

D.1.1
PARTNERSHIP BETWEEN CENTRAL AND LOCAL GOVERNMENT

Underlying all the achievements of the Conservation Programme has been the early establishment and continuity of a good working relationship between the City Council, the Department of the Environment, the Historic Buildings Council and more recently the Historic Buildings and Monuments Commission. The importance of this partnership cannot be overstated and the constant support and encouragement of these various organisations over many years is gratefully acknowledged by the City Council.

The Department of the Environment has provided substantial financial support through all the years of the Programme; and in 1978/79 it positively increased its Section 10 allocation specifically to offset reductions in the City Council's contributions. The Department also adopted a flexible approach to aiding special projects; increasing grant percentages to solve specific problems, for example Nos 2,3 and 4 King's Building [see C.3.1] and Grosvenor Park Baptist Church [see C.9.1], and supporting unusual grant arrangements, such as the scheme for Albion Street [see C.6.0].

Although finance is the most obvious form of support, Chester has also benefited from the expertise and enthusiasm of the Department's and now the Commission's staff. The regular Conservation Programme Progress Meetings are normally attended by an officer from the Commission so that local developments can be discussed and ideas shared. The value of this regular communication can be seen in all that has been achieved.

NO. 5 CASTLE STREET UNDER RESTORATION IN 1983.

D.1.2
RESTORATION AND REPAIR OF
OVER SIX HUNDRED BUILDINGS

The repair and restoration of historic buildings has always been the backbone of the Conservation Programme. It has varied from the spectacular restoration of buildings that were once on the point of collapse, such as The Falcon in Lower Bridge Street, to small grants for the 'loving daily care' of minor buildings. It has been this detailed concern for minor problems which epitomises the Council's approach to historic buildings. Owners and tenants have quickly found that the Council's Conservation Team are concerned about even the smallest difficulty. If a gutter is blocked or a downpipe leaking, it will be drawn to their attention. Advice on appropriate repairs and alterations has always been offered, even where grants were not possible. At the other end of the spectrum, this same concern has led to the full use of the Council's legal powers to purchase buildings in order to ensure their restoration.

Over six hundred buildings have been repaired with the help of grants from central government and the City and County Councils, but the majority of the finance has come from the private sector. This rep-resents a substantial investment in the renewal of both the fabric and the economy of the city, helping to create confidence in the future. Without this postive approach many historic buildings would undoubtedly have been demolished, and the historic character of the district irrevocably lost.

D.1.3
PUBLIC SUPPORT AND CONFIDENCE

The Conservation Programme enjoys general support within the city and the district. It is not politically contentious, being supported by all parties, and receives good press coverage. There is general appreciation of the results of the Programme, the preservation and enhancement of Chester's historic image and the maintenance of an environment that people enjoy.

Public support has been very important. It enables the Council to continue to levy a 'conservation rate', even in times of financial restraint, and encourages efforts to use all the available means to save historic buildings. This includes the possibility of compulsory purchase, although in practice that power has never been fully used. Owners reluctant to carry

SCHOOLCHILDREN WORKING FROM THE CHESTER HERITAGE CENTRE, STUDY BUILDINGS IN ALBION PLACE.

out repairs know that the public is behind the Council and its activities.

The majority of owners have been willing to carry out careful restoration of their properties, involving substantial expenditure from their own pockets. They have also accepted the advice of the Council's Conservation Team and acted accordingly. The success of the Conservation Programme is in no small part the result of the confidence of the public in the Council's policies.

D.1.4
EDUCATION AND THE
HERITAGE CENTRE

An awareness of the need to encourage appreciation of our histroic environment has always been a concern of the Conservation Programme. In 1974 the redundant St Michael's Church in Bridge Street was purchased and converted into the Chester Heritage Centre, with support from the Department of the Environment. It opened in 1975, being the Council's major contribution to European Architectural Heritage Year, and was the first centre of its type in the country. The County Council subsequently converted the Church of St Mary-on-the Hill into an Urban Studies Centre and have recently taken over an important group of warehouses in Duke Street for use as the Cheshire and Diocesan Record Office.

The Heritage Centre is a useful starting point for Chester's many visitors, and also provides a base for many school and college groups studying the city. It houses a permanent exhibition explaining the history of Chester's architecture, encouraging an appreciation of different building materials and techniques, and describing the ongoing Conservation Programme. In 1984/85 over 26,000 people passed through the Centre and five special exhibitions were mounted.

The numerous awards which the Conservation Programme has received [see G.1] have promoted articles in the technical and general press, and the Council's work has been featured in a number of films; notably 'The Conservation Game', produced by the Department of the Environment, and 'Buildings - Who Cares', by the Arts Council and Channel Four Television. The Council have also produced a video 'Chester City - Progress in Conservation' and publish a leaflet, 'Conservation News', three or four times a year, designed to inform the public of current projects. All this has helped to stimulate interest in Chester's historic environment.

OLD AND NEW HOUSING ON THE NORTH SIDE OF KING STREET.

D.1.5
CONSERVATION FINANCE

The concept of a positive 'Conservation Rate' was first accepted in 1969, together with the establishment of a 'Conservation Fund'. Although the special rate has fluctuated over the years, it has always been seen as an identifiable element within the general local authority expenditure.

The purpose of the Conservation Fund, now established under paragraph 16 of the thirteenth schedule of the Local Government Act 1972, as amended, is to encourage and facilitate the conservation of historic buildings, to enhance the appearance of conservation areas; to assist in the payment of fees or charges for providing specialised conservation services; to aid the establishment of Historic Buildings Trusts and the repair of buildings in the control of such trusts; and to finance the publication of conservation reports or literature initiated by the Council.

One of the main advantages of the Fund has been to free the Conservation Programme from the restrictions of 'end of financial year accounting'. The product of the Conservation Rate is paid into the Fund at the beginning of each financial year, and if it is not spent within that year it is held in the fund for future use. This procedure proved useful in the early years when the take-up of grants was very small and the accumulation of the balance provided a buffer against the situation which developed in 1973, when the Programme gained momentum and the number of grant applications increased rapidly. It also enables money to be allocated in advance for very large schemes. For example the restoration of Nos 2, 3 and 4 King's Buildings involved a grant from the City Council of £183,368; and this was accumulated over seven years.

The Council's financial commitment has resulted in substantial funds being made available by central government, through the Historic Buildings Council and its successor, the Historic Buildings and Monuments Commission, This has usually more than doubled the resources available; and without its support, much of what has been achieved would not have been possible.

D.1.6
RESIDENTIAL REGROWTH IN THE CITY CENTRE

Conservation is not just a matter of protecting building fabric. The use of the buildings is equally important and those uses help to determine the character of an area. One of the changes facing historic centres after the Second World War was a steady loss of houses, as people moved out to the suburbs. The implications of this were recognised in Chester by the mid-1960s and policies gradually evolved, both to protect existing houses in the city centre and to create new ones. In 1964 some 3,000 people were living in the centre; but commercial expansion, slum clearance and highway improvements caused this figure to drop to 1,521 by 1971.

Since then the Council's policies have begun to reverse the trend. In the past five

THE PEDESTRIANISATION OF EASTGATE STREET HAS GIVEN PEOPLE THE OPPORTUNITY TO RELAX AND ENJOY THEIR SURROUNDINGS.

years over 280 new dwellings have been constructed within the city centre, approximately half of these being sheltered accommodation for the elderly. A further 50 residential units have been created by the conversion of historic buildings, and many existing houses have been substantially improved. The Greater Chester Local

Plan continues to stress the importance of having people living within the city centre, and wherever possible allocates suitable sites for future housing development.

———

D.1.7
PROGRAMME OF PEDESTRIANISATION

Concern for the quality of the urban spaces around buildings has been evident from the very beginning of the Conservation Programme. The idea of giving priority to pedestrians in the city centre was floated in the Grenfell Baines Plan, 1964. The first moves towards this goal were made in 1972 and the programme has developed continuously ever since.

The present traffic arrangements for the city centre were introduced in March 1981. During extensive public consultation it was clear that some people thought that the scheme did not go far enough, but the requirements for goods deliveries had to be considered. Many traders were genuinely apprehensive about the restrictions; but most agree that it has been good both for them and for the city centre as a whole. Immediately after the start of the experiment there was a slight drop in trade, but within six months, despite a nation-wide economic depression, trade had risen above the levels experienced before pedestrianisation. Since then the number of pedestrians has increased steadily, contributing to the prosperity of the central shopping area.

In order to emphasise the pedestrian priority of the main streets, the Council has introduced new paving, landscaping and seating into Eastgate Street and Northgate Street; and the Historic Buildings and Monuments Commission have provided Section 10 grants for the use of traditional materials in some locations.

The use of expensive materials to complement Chester's buildings and the care taken with the design of the new street furniture represents a very substantial capital investment. However, it makes the centre more attractive for both shoppers and visitors; and is important in constraining the speed of those vehicles which are permitted access. These are now areas where people can enjoy the city, strolling past shops, watching street artists or listening to buskers, admiring the buildings, or just sitting and chatting. Pedestrianisation has not just made the city more visually attractive, it has made its character more human and lively.

———

D.1.8
CONSERVATION INTEGRATED WITH PLANNING

Conservation in Chester is not a marginal or elitist activity, with little relevance to the mainsteam of the Council's activities. Rather it is seen as a fundamental element in planning for the future of the district.

Thus conservation has a central place in both Local Plans covering the Chester District; with concern for the historic environment underlying many of the Council's policies. The Greater Chester Local Plan states that the general structure plan policies are modified for the city centre '...because of the unique character, the level of traffic congestion and the problem of integrating large modern developments into the historic fabric'. Similarly many of the policies relating to the villages in the district revolve around the protection of their historic character.

This integration is also seen in the day to day working of the Council. The Conservation Section are regularly in consultation with other officers, particularly within the Planning Division, but also in many other departments. Comments are made on every planning application that affects a conservation area or listed building, and the Section are just as closely involved in discussions about a new development as in the alteration of a historic building. There is involvement in the implementation and evolution of local plan policies, concern is expressed about dangerous structures and unsatisfactory housing conditions and the managment and maintenance of the Council's own historic buildings is a matter for mutual discussion and action.

For Chester, conservation is a major policy commitment. It is seen as a key element in the economic regeneration of the city and in the creation of a higher quality of life for the residents of the whole district.

THE RUINS OF CAPENHURST HALL

D.2.0
FAILURES

It is not easy to stand back from the detail of the Conservation Programme and to be objective about failures. Everyone has their own personal criticisms of what has happened over the past seventeen years; but it is necessary to remember the background to decisions, why compromises were made, where pressure seemed too strong to resist, why opportunities were missed and consequences not fully explored. This section identifies four broad areas of failure that have resulted in permanent loss or damage to the city and the district. They also represent some of the failures of conservation on a national scale.

D.2.1
OVER-EMPHASIS ON THE CITY CENTRE

During its first five years the Conservation Programme concentrated exclusively on the city centre. This was inevitable, as the work originated with the 1968 Insall Report, which had been commissioned as a study of the central area. Also the national conservation movement was primarily concerned with the problems of historic town centres.

The preparation of the 1976 Review Studies represented the beginning of an appreciation of the problems of conservation in surburban and rural areas. However, progress in this direction has been slow. By 1981 one fifth of the budget was being allocated outside the city centre and it was not until 1986, with a substantial reduction in the Town Scheme, that the suburban and rural areas were allocated as much money as the city centre. Following the completion of the resurvey for a new List of Buildings of Special Architectural or Historic Interest there are now more listed buildings in rural areas than the city centre.

In part, this concentration upon the

centre is a response to its greater problems; but it also reflects a tacit assumption of relative importance, both locally and nationally. Towns are considered to be more important than villages, they have a stronger economic position and their environment is more exciting. Also the returns from expenditure on improving historic town centres can be more easily appreciated in terms of increased tourist or shopping potential. To some extent this is all true, but does it justify an overwhelming emphasis on urban conservation?

The Chester Conservation Programme has concentrated on the city centre partly because of the structure of central government grants for conservation. Town Schemes and Section 10 Schemes operate largely in urban areas because of the need to have some priorities for the use of limited funds, but the historic character of rural villages and isolated listed buildings is equally under threat.

One of the consequences of this concentration upon the city centre is that the Conservation Programme is geared to the restoration of buildings, with less thought being given to preserving other aspects of the environment. Discussions have been held with the Historic Buildings and Monuments Commission about the conservation of rural areas, but further efforts need to be made in this direction.

———

D.2.2
LOSS OF THIRTY LISTED BUILDINGS

Although the Council have generally resisted the demolition of listed buildings, a number have still been lost. In every case this has been because they had reached an advanced state of decay, often with severe structural problems, and representing a genuine danger to the public. Once this point has been reached it becomes difficult to argue a convincing case for their retention and buildings such as Nos 34-42 Lower Bridge Street [see C.5.0] and Nos 32-38 Duke Street [see C.6.0] have been lost. The same problem resulted in the loss of the interior of No. 10 Upper Nortgate Street, although the front facade was successfully retained.

This highlights the importance of regular surveys of the condition of listed

buildings, in order to give advance notice of developing problems. Dereliction and decay need to be identified in good time to allow for effective action. This is a continuous process. Even after a major restoration scheme, there is still a need for regular inspections to identify minor defects, enabling postive action to be taken to prevent serious problems developing.

DERELICT LISTED BUILDINGS IN CUPPIN STREET WHICH HAVE NOW BEEN DEMOLISHED.

———

D.2.3
EDGES OF CONSERVATION AREAS

It is unfortunately true that the drawing of any conservation area boundary immediately reduces the importance of areas outside the line. Less attention is then paid to the detail of planning applications in these areas, specialist advice is not sought or given and less finance is made available. In time this attitude leads to a differential quality of environment along the invisible boundary line, which can also undermine the quality of the conservation area itself. In Chester, such a differential can be appreciated in the area around the Northgate roundabout and along the northern edge of the Boughton and Meadows Conservation Area.

Inevitably, lines have to be drawn around conservation areas but conservation attitudes do not have to be confined. A greater respect for the quality of marginal areas is needed, in order to combat the 'unloved' feeling that is too easily created and to prevent the existence of conservation areas becoming the excuse for environmental damage elsewhere.

D.2.4
INADEQUATE RECORDING OF BUILDINGS

Although over six hundred historic buildings have been repaired with the help of grants, there has been little attempt to record them, or their architectural detail. During repairs much original evidence is often lost or concealed, particularly when buildings have been altered during their history. The work of the Royal Commission on the Historical Monuments of England in recording buildings affected by demolition is excellent, but it cannot cover all the detailed information which comes to light.

Substantial evidence of many buildings built before 1700 has been lost during repair work undertaken as part of the Conservation Programme. This is particularly true of the Rows buildings, many of which contain significant remnants from five or six centuries of development. If a policy of recording while repair work was in progress had been established at the beginning of the Programme, much more would now be known about the development of Chester's buildings. This is now being belatedly recognised. In a letter of November 1984, Brian Antony, Assistant Chief Inspector of the Historic Buildings and Monuments Commission, wrote:

.... I am firmly of the view that the historic buildings in the city should now be properly analysed and recorded. We have directed considerable effort towards repairing them, but it remains true that we know little more about them than we did fifteen years ago.

A project has now been established to survey and record the Rows buildings [see C.1.0], but obtaining finance for this work is difficult. There is still no possibility of even the most basic recording of other buildings as they are altered or repaired.

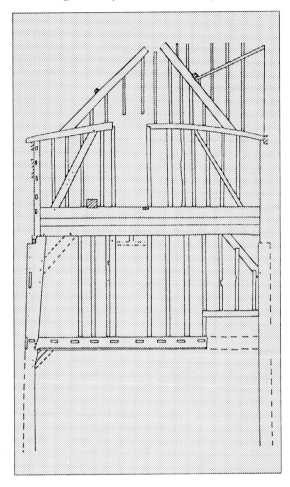

ELEVATION OF INTERNAL WALL, WATERGATE STREET PRODUCED AS PART OF THE ROWS RESEARCH PROJECT.

D.3.0
PROBLEMS

This section identifies those matters of present concern which are thought most likely to be of greatest importance within the Conservation Programme over the next ten years. Areas of opportunity are considered separately [see E.2.0].

D.3.1
THE CONDITION OF HISTORIC BUILDINGS

The success of the Conservation Programme relies upon detailed information on the condition of the district's historic buildings. This is the basis on which decisions about policies, finance, staff time and legal action are taken. Regular surveys of all historic buildings have always been a keynote of the Programme, and this information has been used to direct attention and resources towards priority problem buildings. As is clear from many of the individual case studies [see C], delays in repairing buildings leads to rapidly escalating costs.

Over the past four years the majority of listed buildings in the district have been inspected, together with other key historic buildings. These surveys involved an inspection of the exterior, and in the majority of cases the interior. An approximate estimate of the scale of the problem was made by assessing the cost of necessary repairs and their urgency. The information has been updated and supplemented with reference to the Conservation Section's extensive knowledge of the district. This was particularly necessary in the suburban and rural areas because there has been no systematic survey of building condition in those areas since the new List of Buildings of Special Architectural or Historic Interest was issued.

A significant number of listed buildings are not only in poor condition, but are also considered unfit under the Housing Act 1985. The same is true of some significant unlisted properties in conservation areas. Not only does this indicate that expenditure is required on improvements as well as repairs, it creates the additional problem of satisfying the particular standards of the Housing Act, at the same time as maintaining the character of the building. The size of windows is usually the main problem. Traditional openings seldom allow for the day-lighting or ventilation which are considered necessary for modern housing standards.

All the above information has been used to draw up a list of priority problem buildings and to identify the scale of repairs that are required on historic buildings within the district. In this study, priority problem buildings are those that are estimated to require urgent expenditure of over £15,000; and a total of forty-five such structures have been identified [see G.3]. This is a substantial number and indicates that despite the past seventeen years of intensive activity, more work remains to be done, particularly in the rural area.

D.3.2.
STRUCTURES OF LIMITED ECONOMIC USE

The new List of Buildings of Special Architectural or Historic Interst for the rural area includes a large number of structures with little or no economic use. These include walls, tombs, sign-posts and garden features. Many of these form very significant features within the landscape, and some have great historic and architectural value.

A SEVENTEENTH CENTURY TABLE TOMB IN PLEMSTALL CHURCHYARD.

Any money spent on such structures brings little or no return to the owners, who often consider them to be an embarrassment. Grants are sometimes available from both the City and County Councils but these seldom cover more than a small proportion of the total costs. The maintenance of these structures is simply a matter of investing in future appreciation of the environment. In November 1985 the Council agreed to continue to make the normal levels of grant available to structures of limited economic use; but it may prove necessary to consider increased levels of grant aid in order to encourage the owners to carry out repairs. A number of these structures have been identified as priority problems [see G.4].

D.3.3
DISUSED UPPER FLOORS

The national problem of empty and decaying upper floors was identified in Chester by the 1968 Insall Report; and has had a major place in every other survey of the city centre since. The 1976 Review Study described it as 'intractable'. A 1977 Floorspace Survey of the principal commercial streets in the city centre indicated that there was some 45,000 square metres of vacant or underused space on upper floors in the principal shopping streets, with a further 58,000 square metres of storage space. These figures repesent approximately a quarter of the total floorspace, demonstrating the sheer scale of disuse.

The problem is often of general decay, not only of upper floors, but also of rear extensions. There is no simple or common way of bringing this accommodation back into use. The Chester Rows, with their complex pattern of ownerships and tenancies, create additional problems, and extensive negotiations are generally necessary before even the smallest improvement can be achieved. Following the pilot study of the Watergate Street/Bridge Street block and the 'Stop the Rot' seminar and exhibition in 1981, some progress has been made. A number of buildings have been modified so that their upper floors can be brought into use and this has been greatly assisted by the co-operation of the local fire officers, who understand the difficulties of

———

EMPTY UPPER FLOORS IN CENTRAL CHESTER.

making historic buildings comply with modern fire standards. Plans are being made to improve the access to other buildings.

However the scale of the problem is still substantial. The 1985/86 survey of the city's historic buildings identified twenty-four properties with vacant or underused floor space, of which five are a matter of concern because of their poor condition. Experience shows that the repair and reuse of each of these upper floors will have to be individually promoted and will be a time consuming process.

Chester's backland areas, behind the principal shopping streets, are particularly crowded, with few subsidiary lanes and limited open space. This makes it very difficult to introduce independent accesses to upper floors at the back of buildings. The creation of new pedestrian routes through these areas would assist this process and could be linked to proposals for small scale retail areas [see E.1.1]

———

D.3.4
TRAFFIC MANAGEMENT

The centre of the city demonstrates the problems of integrating cars into a historic environment. The main problem is the congestion of both roads and parking spaces; and the complaints are frequent and predictable. As the character of the urban fabric rests on the tightly-knit nature of narrow streets and contained spaces, any major concesssions to traffic would erode that character. Alternative solutions to relieve the pressure, the development of 'park and ride' schemes, the construction of the Deva Link Road, and a third river crossing may make an impact in the long term, but are beyond the scope of this study. There are, however, smaller aspects of the problem which have implications for the quality of the environment.

After the road surface of King Street had been reinstated with setts, there was a public outcry at the reappearance of the double yellow lines. As more money is spent improving the spaces between buildings, particularly with the use of traditional or good modern materials, it will become less acceptable to use this method to control parking. It has proved possible to dispense with yellow lines in pedestrianised areas such as Eastgate Street, where vehicles entry is restricted and it is obvious by street design and materials that vehicles are intruding into a special area. A similar approach in Northgate Street, in front of the library, has proved less successful, with many drivers complaining about the absence of yellow lines when prosecuted for parking offences. Small paving blocks and signs provide insufficient information when access to the area is unrestricted.

Yellow lines are especially obtrusive on cobbled surfaces, and it is also difficult to apply them to such an uneven surface. The City Council have been particularly keen to find an alternative way of indicating parking restrictions on the cobbled surfaces of St Mary's Hill and Shipgate Street. The County Council have agreed to prohibit waiting on the whole length of these streets and it is hoped that the Department of Transport will agree to this order being implemented without yellow lines.

The provision of adequate parking for people living in the city centre is a growing problem. The Council's policy of encourag-

ing city centre housing, along with improvements to adjacent housing areas, will increase the pressure for some solution to be found. The Council is committed to the introduction of resident's parking schemes, but these have proved difficult to implement. To use front gardens and rear yards is both unsightly and destructive; being carried out with no consideration of the visual impact. In November 1984, in response to the visual chaos that this activity was creating in The Groves, the Council agreed to apply for an Article 4 Direction, enabling it to control the detailed design of new parking spaces in the front gardens [see C.8.0]. The increasing effect of this practice needs to be continuously monitored and urgent action is needed to improve areas already heedlessly damaged by the pressures for parking.

D.3.5
CHURCHES AND CHAPELS

Churches are an outstanding category of buildings with great heritage value, and the district has examples of interest from the medieval period, the seventeenth century and the Gothic Revival. A total of 56 churches, including a number of Nonconformist churches and chapels, are on the List of Buildings of Special Architectural or Historic Interest; thirteen Grade I and twenty Grade II*. Even churches and chapels which are not listed tend to make a very important contribution to the environment, as a result of their distinctive presence.

Churches are costly to repair and maintain, both because of their size and because of the materials and details that were used. In modern functional terms they are often unnecessarily large for their usage; but it is not generally appropriate to suggest that congregations should move to more practical and economic premises. Having to find a new use for the building would in any case produce a greater conservation problem. Churches are a particularly difficult type of building to adapt to a different use, especially when both the building and the interior furnishings are of historic interest.

The best conservation approach to churches and chapels is to try and maintain them for religious use. Interestingly, in

ST OSWALD'S CHURCH RISING ABOVE CHURCH STREET, MALPAS.

the past few years two redundant churches in the city centre, which looked as though they would pose problems of reuse, have found new religious use through different Christian sects.

The cost of offering grants to congregations to maintain their churches and thus to keep them in use, is high. Table Two sets out the grants that have been made by the Council and central government over the past six years. It is noticeable that the figures for the last three years are significantly higher than for the first three years. This probably reflects both an increasing awareness by congregations of the need to maintain their buildings and also an increased knowledge of the available grants. On average during the past three years, just over 10% of the Conservation Fund has been spend on grants to churches, but these figures include the exceptional grants to the former Grosvenor Park Baptist Church [see C.9.1] and are therefore slightly misleading. Nevertherless the proportion of the Conservation Fund that is spent on church repairs needs to be monitored, to ensure that it is not disproportionately high.

D.3.6
HISTORIC RURAL AREAS

The conservation of historic rural areas involves many different agencies. The general deterioration of historic landscapes and the pressures for change threaten archaeological remains, field patterns, ancient trackways, woodlands and hedgerows, flora and fauna, parklands, historic buildings and garden features. These are the concerns of, and are affected by, many different agencies. The County Council in particular has made significant efforts to conserve the landscape of the district, having built up a wide range of skills and relationships over the past two decades. The present allocation of finance from the Conservation Fund towards the rural areas is only helping in one area of this complex problem; the restoration of buildings. There is a need to give greater consideration to the wider aspects of rural conservation.

Although the various pressures are caused by many different factors, the most significant is agriculture - an industry in an uncertain and changing state. The majority of farmers have grown up during a period when they were given every encourage-

TABLE TWO
GRANTS TO CHURCHES IN CHESTER DISTRICT 1980/86

	1980/1	1981/2	1982/3	1983/4	1984/5	1985/6
CITY COUNCIL	7,889	3,389	3,716	28,325	15,244	21,241
DOE/HBMC OUTSTANDING CHURCHES GRANTS	2,366	1,099	—	21,591	—	4,792
DOE/HBMC SECTION 10 GRANTS	1,184	5,261	—	34,810	14,105	15,648

ISOLATED COTTAGES IN EDGE.

ment to increase productivity and they are now having to adapt to changing rules. There is encouragement to find alternative ways of producing income from the land; and it is becoming recognised that conservation, forestry, leisure and tourism provide major alternatives. The rethinking of agricultural policies and attitudes provides an opportunity to develop policies which will encourage the conservation of sensitive historic rural areas.

In May 1986 the City and County Councils organised a day seminar to discuss the general problems and opportunities of historic landscapes. It was attended by representatives of many of the organisations who are concerned with the countryside, including farmers and land agents. Although there was no attempt during the seminar to achieve agreement on the result of the discussion, a number of common themes did emerge:

1. There was general support from all groups for the encouragement of conservation in historic rural areas.

2. Key areas of historic importance should be identified and detailed policies prepared for those areas - rather than general policies for wide areas. These policies should be agreed with the landowners and farmers concerned, so that they can be implemented as part of management agreements, using existing resources.

3. There are so many different organisations involved with rural conservation that the appointment of a project officer/co-ordinator to provide a single local contact for advice and resources should be investigated. This might be achieved with joint funding from bodies such as the Countryside Commission and the Development Commission.

4. The possibility of establishing new initiatives for the repair and use of historic buildings should be investigated, probably requiring a rolling fund with finance from a wide variety of organisations. This might also include arrangements for the management of different uses, such as holiday accommodation.

D.3.7
REDUNDANT FARM BUILDINGS

The new List of Buildings of Special Architectural or Historic Interest has helped to identify the importance of buildings in the countryside. The majority of these are farmhouses with associated farm buildings, which often stand in isolation from the main villages or hamlets. Such locations make them very important within the overall landscape.

Modern farming practices, involving increased mechanisation, have radically altered the size and form of the farm buildings required. Many traditional structures with their narrow spans and small openings are falling into marginal use or becoming totally redundant. If they are to be retained for the sake of their intrinsic importance or their landscape significance, new uses have to be found.

Within the district a total of 167 farm buildings are listed, together with 78 farm buildings. There is some overlap between the two groups, but approximately 200 groups of farm buildings include one or more which are listed. Only a proportion include redundant buildings, but it is a growing proportion.

The Chester Rural Area Local Plan recognises the problems; and states that there will be a presumption in favour of alternative employment uses in redundant buildings. An associated policy states that structures that are of architectural or historic interest, are associated with a listed building, or make a valuable contribution to the character of the rural area may be converted for residential use. Applications for conversion to employment uses

A REDUNDANT EIGHTEENTH CENTURY DOVECOT, NOW RESTORED, AT DODLESTON HALL FARM.

since 1979 have fluctuated each year; there is no discernable trend and none of the applications have related to listed structures. In contrast, applications for residential conversion have been increasingly popular and a significant proportion have been for the conversion of listed farm buildings or were adjacent to a listed farmhouse.

Residential conversions of farm buildings do represent a fundamental change of character. Extensive alterations, such as the sub-division of the interior and the insertion of new windows are inevitable; as is the transformation of hard surfaced farmyards into gardens. This is particularly noticeable when they are converted into a number of residential units, and even the most sensitive of schemes leads to an unavoidable change of character.

The Local Plan policy states that a residential use will normally be acceptable providing it '....will not materially affect the architectural or historic interest of the building'. In important, but unlisted buildings the interest is in the overall form, massing and materials, rather than in individual details or interior spaces; therefore the changes involved in residential conversion are generally acceptable. This is not true of listed buildings, which have intrinsic architectural and historic interest. At least one listed farm building in the district was excluded from the new List of Buildings of Special Architectural or Historic Interest partly because of its residential

conversion. Too great a change had occurred for it to qualify, despite a sensitive conversion scheme.

Conversion to employment uses generally involves minimal alterations and is therefore more successful in retaining the traditional character. It would therefore be appropriate for the Council to adopt a policy of favouring light industrial or office uses for listed farm buildings. Such a policy would be assisted by the Rural Development Area status of the southern section of the district, which enables grants to be made for the conversion of buildings for employment purposes. There will be some circumstances, often related to location, which make such uses unsuitable and in these cases residential use might still be accepted if that appeared to be the only way of preserving the building.

D.3.8
DESIGN

One of the major factors that mobilised public opinion in favour of conservation during the 1960s was the way new buildings were ignoring the traditional scale and texture of historic cities. The Pepper Street elevation of the Grosvenor Precinct and the eight storey block of Commerce House in Hunter Street are often quoted as examples of the failure of architects, developers and planners to produce buildings of quality, sympathetic to their settings.

Inevitably, part of the problem is the increasing size of new developments. This is a historic trend which has to be accepted. One recent solution has been to design developments such as Heritage Court in Lower Bridge Street, that look like a group of separate buildings and incorporate replica facades of the previous buildings. This may be appropriate in certain cases, but it can too easily become a false front trying to disguise the bulk of the building behind.

Design concepts are changing; and recent schemes such as No 12 Watergate Street and No 20 Grosvenor Street show that new developments can be sympathetic to the existing character of the city. However, these two buildings rely heavily on the details of the past. Chester has

ATTRACTIVE ESTATE COTTAGES WITH 'GOTHICK' WINDOWS AT CREWE NEAR FARNDON.

extremely few good late twentieth century buildings, honestly 'modern' and making their own contribution to the variety of architectural styles which form the character of the city. The C & A Building in Foregate Street, designed in 1970, is still probably the best in this category.

As Chester enters what may prove to be another period of redevelopment, the problem of encouraging good design for new buildings is crucial. The Council, as the local planning authority, should encourage good modern designs that can stand alongside Chester's historic buildings. This is equally true for the city and the outlying areas. In particular, the design of new housing is often abysmally low, both in speculative and purpose built schemes. This can be seen especially when they are set against the simple well-proportioned cottages of the nineteenth century and the inspired inventiveness of the vernacular revival buildings, which make up so many of the district's villages.

Design problems are also evident in the small scale alterations and extensions which comprise the majority of planning applications. The general level of shopfront and advertising design is particularly poor; and the majority of retailers appear to have little idea of the value of design. Substantial sums are spent on refurbishing shop units, yet time and again the new external appearance is only marginally different from the previous mediocre attempt or the boring efforts of competitors.

Unfortunately, encouraging good design is difficult. It is too often thought to be only a matter of taste, and therefore not a legitimate area for control. Apart from education, suggesting the use of a good designer and giving awards to the better designs, refusing planning permission for the worst examples is the only available course of action. This will still allow the mediocre, the 'barely acceptable' developments to continue.

D.3.9
CRAFTSMANSHIP

During the past seventeen years the City Council's Conservation Team have been involved in what seems like a continual and sometimes losing battle with architects, surveyors, engineers and builders over appropriate methods of repairing and altering historic buildings. Although there are a few individuals who are sympathetic to the sensitive nature of historic structures, the majority seem to have little understanding of traditional building materials and methods. This is exacerbated by the unwillingness of owners to pay for craftmanship.

There is a general eagerness to replace rather than repair, to use modern materials rather than traditional methods and to accept cheapness as an acceptable alterna-

A SIMPLE NINETEENTH CENTURY COTTAGE OF LOCAL BRICK IN
TATTENHALL.

tive to quality. When this attitude is allied to builders who simply do not know how to carry out traditional techniques, even when they are specified, the chances of sympathetic repair are slim.

Chester has suffered particularly from poor and bad repointing of brickwork. The majority of the historic brickwork is composed of either a soft weathered brick or a hard Ruabon brick, often laid with very narrow joints. Both take a little skill in handling, but it is seldom seen. There is also a general shortage of joiners with the skill and understanding necessary to repair timber framed buildings.

In addition, there are problems with crafts which have been neglected over the past fifty years. Chester is suffering from an increasing shortage of competent stone-

BAD
RE-POINTING.

masons, which will shortly create a serious problem for repairs to the City Walls and the majority of the historic churches.

These problems stem from a failure of education at all levels. Many owners do not appreciate the long term advantages of a well crafted repair. Surprisingly few architects or engineers have received more than a passing reference to traditional building techniques during their long professional education. The training of builders in anything other than the very basic skills seems to be a thing of the past. However, what is possibly more serious is that communication on the actual site is lacking. The techniques are not specified, or if specified a poorer quality of work is accepted. Until the traditional techniques are taught, specified and nothing less is accepted, these problems will continue.

A few years ago a 'Guild of Restorers' was proposed, to train craftsmen and to carry out repairs. The Guild hoped to start with the training of stonemasons because it was already apparent that this skill was fast disappearing. The project failed to materialise, but in view of the continuing problems it might be an idea worth pursuing again. The Council could, for example, join with the Cathedral and the Chester Diocesan Board, to promote a training programme based on practical repair work to the many buildings and structures owned by those organisations.

WATERGATE STREET IN 1970.

E

FUTURE CONTEXT

It seems to us that, to reduce Chester to an imitation of some third-rate quarter of the

metropolis is as great a piece of folly on the part of its magnates as the killing of the goose

that laid the golden eggs.... The thousands of visitors who are attracted to Chester by the

beauty of its street architecture must surely be an item worthy of consideration.

Diminish this attraction and one great source of traffic will disappear.

The Builder,
1865

E

FUTURE CONTEXT

———

THE CONSERVATION Programme is only part of the continuing development of Chester as a place with something special to offer - an attractive district, with an image which will draw in people and investment. The 1968 Insall Report comments:

Chester's prosperity will depend ultimately on its ability to attract the region's custom, and this it can do not only by the variety of its goods but by making the best use of its environmental advantages.

Conservation policies cannot be considered in isolation. They are closely identified with the commercial and social life of the area. Before discussing specific opportunities, resources and proposals, it is appropriate to examine those activities that reply upon the image of the district; its economic success in terms of shopping and tourism, and its appeal from a residential standpoint.

———

E.1.0
THE ECONOMIC LIFE
OF THE DISTRICT

Chester has experienced a varied economic history. During the thirteenth and fourteenth centuries, it was a major international port, but its importance declined during the fifteenth century as a result of the silting of the River Dee. By the eighteenth century, the creation of new harbours further down the estuary had helped to maintain the city as an important trading link with Ireland. This role was lost with the development of Liverpool and Holyhead during the nineteenth century; and Chester had to rely upon its position as a centre of communication, based initially on coaches and the canal, and later on the railways.

The city has always been a regional centre, but twenty years ago even that was in question. Major developments in Liverpool, the creation of New Towns at Warrington, Runcorn and Telford, and the construction of a new road network bypassing the city, could all have adversely affected the economic life of Chester.

In the event Chester has maintained and strengthened its position in the region. It is an established service centre; 75% of all jobs in the district being within this sector. Public services are of greatest significance, demonstrating the city's role as a 'county

THE MODERN CATHEDRAL BELL TOWER.

town'. Local Government, branch offices of central government, further education, statutory bodies, health authorities etc, together account for an estimated 28% of all jobs within the district.

Of most significance for the future are those sectors of employment which are most likely to change. The future of the public sector is uncertain and will be dependant upon political decisions. Agriculture is in decline as a source of employment, and construction and transport seem unlikely to show any significant change in the foreseeable future. The main areas of employment that are open to change are manufacturing [17% of jobs at present], distribution and catering [25%] and the private service market [10%]. If these sectors of its employment market are to expand, Chester has to be in a position to attract people and investment. It is competing directly with other cities and therefore needs to be able to offer something different, something over and above other areas.

The greatest of the district's primary assets is its 'prestige' image as an attractive area; both city and surrounding countryside. The value of this is difficult to quantify but it is undoubtedly that extra factor which gives Chester an edge on its competitors. Researchers, investigating alternative areas for the location of new offices, say that Chester's image makes relocating employees to the area an attractive proposition. The high standard of the environment will be an important factor in the district's economic growth. Care and improvement of this environment needs to be freed from the defensive stance in which it is so often cast and to be seen instead as a postive way of promoting employment.

——

E.1.1.
SHOPPING

In relation to its population, Chester has a very high sales turnover. This can be mainly attributed to the wide catchment area of the city, which includes the Wirral, a large part of Cheshire and a substantial area of North Wales. It also extends to North Shropshire and draws from Liverpool and Manchester. This attraction

THE OLDEST SHOP FRONTAGE IN THE COUNTRY.

——

is maintained, despite the frequent complaints about the city's resultant car parking difficulties.

Chester's success as a shopping centre appears to rest on three elements: the quality and variety of the shops; the compact nature of the centre, which is assisted by the double level shopping in the Rows; and the historic environment. A report by Schiller and Jarrett, in 'Land Development Studies', 1985, ranked Chester as the top non-metropolitan shopping centre in the country. It also indicated that over the past few years, Chester, together with other historic cities, had improved its ranking relative to other shopping centres.

Some of the present national trends in retailing could threaten Chester's shopping centre, but other changes may be beneficial. Over the past forty years, regional distinctions and specialities have disappeared and national multiples are dominant. The high rentals in many of Chester's shopping areas encourage this trend, since few local retailers can compete. This is already reducing the variety of the shops. The trend towards 'out of town' stores and shopping centres may also threaten the economic life of the city centre. The opportunities for larger stores with easy access and car parking makes for convenience, but may draw a proportion of sales from the traditional centre, reducing turnover and discouraging new investment.

In contrast, the expansion of speciality retailing, appealing to a leisure and tourist market, could benefit the city. Such an approach was indicated in the Grenfell Baines Plan, 1964, which recommended that:

...the City Council take active steps to sponsor small scale 'special' shops at low rentals and deliberately create something that is different.

This is an area of growth which is particularly appropriate for historic cities but it may require positive support from the Council. A report on the Council of

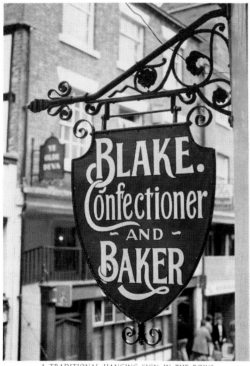

A TRADITIONAL HANGING SIGN IN THE ROWS.

Europe Congress on European Architectural Heritage, held in Amsterdam in 1975, observed:

...it is hoped that the incentive of conservation grants can be used to encourage the retention of small traders whose presence is such a vital factor in the continuing success of our City.

Eastgate Street Row North and Bridge Street Row West are both areas which would benefit from positive encouragement of specialist retail uses. There are also opportunities behind both sides of Bridge Street for the development of small scale retail areas, similar in character to Godstall Lane [see C.1.0].

E.1.2
TOURISM

While tourism can be influenced by good marketing, it is important to note that the basic environmental quality of town and countryside alike is often what attracts the tourist in the first place.

This observation was made by Jim Morrissey in an article, 'Tourism and the Public Sector', The Planner, June 1986. Chester's economic life relies heavily on the success of the city as a tourist centre. It was estimated that in 1983 visitors spent £38 million in the city, and that at least 4,000 jobs were directly related to the tourist industry. This is closely linked to the maintenance of an historic image, as the Visitors in Chester Study 1984, commented:

This historic heritage, which over the past 10 to 15 years has been the subject of the City Council's extensive and ambitious conservation and restoration programme, is undoubtedly the prime resource for tourism in the city.

Many visitors come only for the day, inevitably spending most of their time at the major attractions; City Walls, Rows, Cathedral and River. Over-night visitors represent under a fifth of the total, but they make a much higher contribution to the local economy. Interestingly, the majority of these staying visitors also spend the whole of their time in the city centre, few having any intention of visiting attractions in the surrounding area.

The Visitors in Chester Study concluded that "....Chester had by no means reached capacity as far as visitor numbers are concerned". However, it is recognised that there is a concentration of visitors in certain limited areas, such as the Cross, Eastgate Street and the Cathedral, while other attractions are under-utilised. In particular, visitors are unable to have access to some buildings of major historic interest, such as Bishop Lloyd's Palace. The study has recommended spreading the load. The existing attractions are not managed to advantage and they need to be developed within the framework of a comprehensive tourism policy.

E.1.3
RESIDENTIAL APPEAL

The city and its surrounding villages provide a highly attractive residential environment. This is an important asset in the district's ability to attract new employment activites. In recent years the advantages of living close to the amenities of a centre such as Chester have been rediscovered. This has led to increasing demand for the traditional houses of the inner suburbs and has reinforced the Council's policy of increasing residential provision within the city centre [see D.1.6].

Chester District is part of a very complex pattern of employment. Almost 40% of its jobs are filled by residents from Clwyd, Wirral and the rest of Cheshire, at least in part because of Chester's growing role as a major service centre. Conversely, approximately 30% of the district's residents work in surrounding areas, in manufacturing industries which do not exist within the district. This latter figure is a significant proportion for a district which provides so many jobs. It is largely the result of the attractive environment provided for people willing to commute to adjacent centres of employment. This is part of a regional trend, with middle and upper income groups moving into areas around the southern edges of the Liverpool and Manchester conurbations. There is a resulting influence on house-prices, with a particular demand for high value housing.

Chester benefits from people who choose to live within the district even when they work elsewhere. The high stand-

ATTRACTIVE HOUSES IN TATTENHALL.

ard of the historic environment is particularly attractive to the more prosperous people of the region. Companies proposing to move their operations from the South-East are often concerned that their staff should be able to maintain their housing investment, and the existence of appropriately priced housing is an important factor in their choice of location. Thus the district's residential appeal helps to attract new commercial investment, not only to Chester, but also to the wider area.

———

E.2.0
OPPORTUNITIES

The section on the problems facing conservation [see D.3.0] has begun to suggest appropriate policies for the future, but policies should not be determined only by problems. There must be a willingness to grasp opportunities and to create initiatives.

In July 1985 the Council implemented a programme of detailed conservation area studies, to supplement the basic policy framework of the Local Plans; identifying the need for additional controls and opportunties for enhancement. The study of Tattenhall Conservation Area is now complete and a leaflet will be published in the near future. Work is in progress on the Elton, Malpas, Stoak and Thornton-le-Moors Conservation Areas.

This section looks beyond the immediate problems and identifies directions in which positive action now will be of substantial benefit in the future. Although generally these initiatives will come from the Council, conservation is a co-operative activity, so the proposals will rely upon the active support of many other bodies and individuals.

———

E.2.1.
SPECIAL GRANT SCHEMES FOR HISTORIC BUILDINGS

The Chester Town Scheme is well established and has been so successful that its work is nearly completed. The Section 10 schemes for Shotwick and Boughton Riverside, operated in conjunction with the Historic Buildings and Monuments Commission, are now more easily understood as small scale, special schemes. Other areas would benefit from similar initiatives if the funds are available.

An application in 1984 for a Section 10 scheme for Elton was refused by the Commission because of the marginal quality of the conservation area and because they considered there to be no scope for a scheme of repairs [see C.11.3]. Yet it is precisely these problems that place the character of the historic core of the village at risk.

As the emphasis of the Council's Conservation Programme has shifted towards activity outside the city centre, there has been an increasing divergence of opinion between the Council and the Commission. In part this is inevitable. Chester City Centre is accepted as being of national importance, but some of the surrounding areas are little different from the majority of the county. The Commission is

————

RESTORATION WORK ON VICARAGE FARM, SHOTWICK.

a national body and has to direct its resources on the basis of national priorities. Nevertheless, there is concern, not only in Chester, that the Commission's limited resources prevent greater consideration being given to the national importance of historic buildings outside towns and cities.

The Council should continue to identify areas which would benefit from special grant schemes and to press both the Commission and central government to make more funds available for such

schemes. It may also be necessary to investigate the possibility of support from other bodies.

————

E.2.2
CONSERVING THE LANDSCAPE

Over the past seventeen years, the main concern of the Conservation Programme has been the restoration of buildings, with a growing interest in the quality of the spaces between buildings. However the conservation of the landscape is of similar importance, both as an historic feature in its own right and as the setting for individual buildings, villages and the city itself.

The Council's Local Plans have stressed the importance of the Green Belt around the city, and of other landscape areas:

An important aspect of the character of the City is the open areas and woodland which, in places form green 'wedges' separating the old part of the city from its suburbs. These areas provide a landscape setting for the City and secure a relationship between the built environment and the open countryside.

The need to maintain these areas and to encourage replanting is mentioned, but a positive approach is required to ensure that action is taken. Key areas of deteriorating landscape must be identified and agreement reached with landowners on policies for management and replanting. This work has to be given priority, since replanting needs to be carried out on a regular basis before the existing trees die. In many cases it is already too late to avoid a time gap in the tree landscape. The County Council are active in this field [see D.3.6] and co-operation between the two authorities could reinforce what is already being achieved.

————

E.2.3
ENVIRONMENTAL IMPROVEMENTS

The Council's programme of pedestrianisation has already been described [see D.1.7] but there are still areas of major opportunity. Following the completion of the repaving of the Town Hall Square and the area in front of the Forum, the original programme proposed similar treatment for Bridge Street and Watergate Street, to enhance their shopping potential. The improvements to The Groves also need to be extended along to the Old Dee Bridge.

The Council have sought to retain and repair traditional street materials and have obtained an agreement with the County Council, as the highway authority, on appropriate materials for repairs to pavements in the city centre. The reinstatement of the traditional surface materials in King Street [see C.3.0] has demonstrated the value of this type of improvement for minor streets. There are a number of other streets, such as Bunce Street, Castle Street and Whitefriars, that would benefit from a similar approach and which might well be eligible for Section 10 grants.

The Visitors in Chester Study suggested that there was scope for substantial improvement in the visual impact of some areas. The City Centre may be the 'jewel of the north-west', but it has also been described as a jewel in a very grubby setting. There are many forgotten areas, left over after other developments have taken place; and a number of these are on the main approaches to the city centre.

Many of the village conservation areas are spoilt by extensive displays of overhead wiring. Tarvin Civic Trust have been particularly concerned about this problem; and Dunham-on-the-Hill, Farndon and Shotwick are also badly affected. The cost of putting wiring underground is high, but in key areas the visual benefits would be substantial. It may also be appropriate to co-ordinate undergrounding with improvements to paved surfaces.

There are many opportunities to achieve small environmental improvements in the urban and rural conservation areas. The Tattenhall Conservation Area Study [see E.2.0] has identified a number of possibilities, such as tree and hedge planting, changes in colour schemes, repair of minor features and improvements to signs. Similar opportunities exist in other areas.

For some of these improvements, the bulk of the expenditure will have to be met by the Council, while for others it may be possible to arrange joint funding with other bodies. For minor improvements, small

SETTS AND COBBLES IN BRIDGE PLACE WERE REPAIRED IN 1972.

FINGERPOST AT THE CROSS

grants to local groups or private individuals may be a sufficient 'pump-priming' mechanism.

E.2.4

TOURIST POTENTIAL

The relationship between tourism and conservation has already been mentioned [see E.1.2]. The effect of the Conservation Programme over the past seventeen years has been to maintain and enhance Chester's image as a historic city which attracts many visitors.

Many projects already in hand or proposed contain a tourism element, although this may not be the main reason for their implementation. These include the pedestrian paving in the city centre, the improvement to The Groves, the proposals for City Road and the Station forecourt, the work around the Northgate Locks and the floodlighting programme. It is also important for the Council to regularly update the displays in the museum and Heritage Centre so as to maximise the appeal of these assets.

Tourist potential is not restricted to the city centre. Much of the district is attractive countryside with many areas of interest. Some of the problem historic buildings in the rural area might find new uses as holiday accommodation. From these, and from the city, it would be possible to encourage exploration of the area, through the use of good interpretative material. There are a number of landscaped parks of historic interest within the district, but none of them are regularly open to the public. The development of one of them as a country park or garden could provide a focal point for extended visits within the rural area.

There are obviously many opportunities which could be developed to enhance Chester's tourist potential, but these need to be considered within an overall strategy for tourism [see E.1.2]. However, the buildings themselves suggest certain possibilities, particularly within the city, where there are five principal monuments or groups of buildings of major historic interest:

i. The City Walls

The City Walls are the outstanding historic feature of Chester. The Romans appear to have rebuilt their military camp towards the end of the second century and this probably included the construction of a stone perimeter wall. The defences of the settlement were later extended to the south and west. The Walls have been extensively rebuilt and altered over the centuries, and the original defensive function has been adapted to form an almost continuous high level pedestrian walkway.

The Walls are of interest in their own right, but they also provide an interesting route around the city, linking many of the areas of historic interest. This aspect could be exploited, as a 'necklace' strategy, with the wall as the thread and the attractions as beads. Such an approach would require good signposting, and this would assist in reinforcing the continuity of the walls, which is relatively weak on the western section.

The historic interest of the Walls would be considerably enhanced by the use of good interpretative material, possibly including explanatory plaques in key positions. Additional lighting and some

THE ROWS ON THE NORTH SIDE OF EASTGATE STREET.

seats would be of benefit and opportunities should be taken to improve the views, both of and from the Walls [see C.7.0].

ii. The Cathedral and Abbey Buildings

Chester Cathedral contains work from many different periods, but the dominant impression is that created by the Victorian restorers, notably Sir George Gilbert Scott. The Cathedral is also part of a substantial group of monastic and secular buildings; the cloisters, its surrounding ranges including the chapter house and refectory, the eighteenth century developments of Abbey Square and Abbey Street, and the late nineteenth century buildings built for the King's School on the site of the Bishop's Palace.

This group of buildings is already a major tourist attraction and on some busy days reaches its capacity to absorb visitors. It may be possible to regulate visitors by developing other areas of the cathedral precinct; increasing its capacity to absorb visitors, without creating congestion and damage.

iii. The Rows

The Visitors in Chester Study identifies congestion on the Rows, particularly Eastgate Street Row South, as the area most likely to create difficulties between visitors, residents and traders. Conversely there are stretches of the Rows which are very underused. The Council have taken action to try and increase the economic attractiveness of these underused areas [see C.1.0] and it may also be appropriate to give some thought to their tourist potential.

The Chester Rows Research Project [see C.1.0] is beginning to demonstrate that Chester has probably one of the most important groups of historic town houses in the country. For example, Watergate Street contains good examples from every century, from the thirteenth to the twentieth. In co-operation with the owners of a selection of these buildings, it would be possible to develop a town house trail. This would not need to involve turning each house into a museum. Many of the buildings are already accessible to the public as shops or offices, and the introduction of interpretative material would be sufficient to stimulate interest.

iv. The Castle

Chester Castle was founded by William the Conqueror, and provided Edward I with his base for the conquest of North Wales. Little now remains of what must have been an impressive medieval structure; and only from the south does the

121

complex of buildings fit most people's image of a castle. The majority of the site is occupied by Thomas Harrison's extensive complex of Court and military buildings, erected between 1788 and 1822. Nikolaus Pevsner described them as '...one of the most powerful monuments of the Greek Revival in the whole of England'.

The castle is under-utilised as an attraction, yet it could stimulate tourist activity in the south-west corner of the city. The Historic Buildings and Monuments Commission, who are responsible for the oldest buildings, intend to improve access and display over the next few years. The setting of the castle and access to the inner bailey could also be substantially improved.

v. Roman Amphitheatre

The site of the Roman Amphitheatre was identified in 1929 during the construction of an extension to the Dee House Convent. Following extensive reorganisation of the road proposals for the area, the excavation and consolidation of the northern half of the amphitheatre was completed in 1972. It is the largest of the two stone amphitheatres so far discovered in Britain, and is probably the most architecturally sophisticated.

The proposed sale of the convent buildings by British Telecom may allow excavation of the southern half of the amphitheatre so that the whole monument can be appreciated. If such a scheme included an imaginative interpretation centre, the city would gain a further major attraction. The fully excavated amphitheatre could be the setting for a variety of different events during the summer. Such a proposal would act as a focal point for an extensive recreational area in the southeast corner of the city. A network of pedestrian routes could link the amphitheatre to the Roman Gardens, the City Walls, St. John's Church and The Groves.

E.3.0
RESOURCES

The District's historic character, its buildings, streets, villages and landscape, is a resource with an immense reputation for attractiveness, contributing to the

CHESTER CASTLE

economic vitality of the area. These assets need to be conserved, used and enjoyed if the district is to continue to benefit from them. In order to develop practical policies for the future, the resources that are available to solve the problems and to grasp the opportunities need to be assessed.

E.3.1
FINANCE

Most of the money for conservation comes from the private sector. The grants made available from both central and local government are intended as 'pump-primers', to help encourage owners to carry out appropriate repairs. This policy has proved remarkably economic and effective, currently resulting in the investment of over £1 million in the restoration of the

THE WATER TOWER

District's buildings each year. Since 1970, some 400 city centre buildings, 50 urban and 200 rural buildings have been extensively repaired. Without grant aid many important buildings would undoubtedly have been lost, and the historic character of the area irrevocably changed.

i. City Council Finance

Table Three shows the Council's allocations to the Conservation Fund since 1970, in both monetary and real terms. The increase up to 1975/76, the cutback in the late 1970s and the reinstatement of the real value of the fund in 1980/81 are all apparent.

The effectiveness of the Conservation Fund has been increased by the decision in 1982 to reduce the percentage of the grant normally given under the Town Scheme from 50% to 40% [20% from City Council, 20% from HBMC]. This did not appear to adversely affect the implementation of grant aided repairs; and a further reduction to 30% was introduced for the financial year 1986/87. These decisions demonstrate how the grants given over the past seventeen years have improved property values and the general confidence of the private sector in the city centre.

The 1976 Review Study recommended that the Conservation Fund should

TOWN HALL, NORTHGATE STREET.

be reviewed and rolled forward on a three year basis. This idea was adopted and has proved invaluable in planning large repair schemes, which have to be organised over a number of years. Without an ongoing commitment beyond the end of a single financial year, it would prove difficult to persuade owners to start major repair

TABLE THREE
CITY COUNCIL'S ALLOCATIONS TO CONSERVATION FUND 1970/87

▦ Interest accrued to Conservation Fund

☐ Allocation to Conservation Fund

■ Real value of allocation related to 1970/1 costs, based on Building Cost Indices

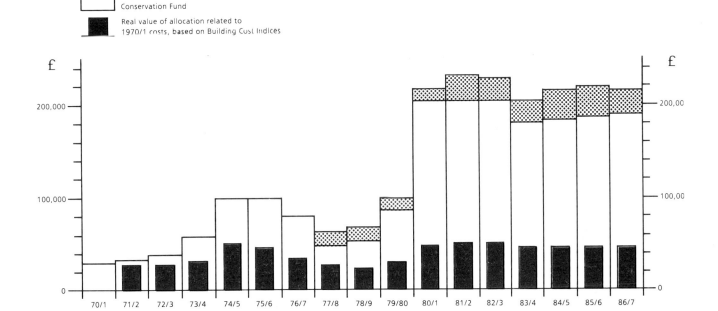

schemes. A number of special grant schemes, such as the Town Scheme and the Boughton Riverside Section 10 Scheme, have equally to be planned as a commitment for a number of years so as to attract matching funds from the Historic Buildings and Monuments Commission.

At the beginning of each financial year the Conservation Fund monies are allocated between four main budget heads. Table Four shows the relative expenditure in each area over the past six years:

[a] CITY TOWN SCHEME BUDGET - to match the contribution of the Historic Buildings and Monuments Commission towards the Town Scheme in the City Conservation Area. Grants from this budget have remained reasonably constant over the past five years. The majority of problem buildings have now been restored; the virtual completion of works in the Bridgegate Action Area and the restoration of 2-4 Kings Buildings representing the major successes of recent years. As a result, the Council has agreed with the Historic Buildings and Monuments Commis-

sion that the three year Town Scheme for 1986/89 should be reduced to £60,000 per annum from each party.

Twenty priority problem buildings have been identified within the City Centre Conservation Area [see G.3] but some of these would not be eligible for Town Scheme grant. A further 104 buildings were judged to require repair within five years. The present three year Town Scheme will end in March 1989. From present information it seems unlikely that a continuation of the scheme beyond that date can be justified to the Commission. There will however be a small residual need for grant aid in the City Conservation Area, partly connected with upper floor schemes. From all this information it has been possible to assess the likely minimum need for grants up to 1991/92 [see Tables Five and Six].

[b] CITY NON-TOWN SCHEME BUDGET - to provide grants for buildings within the City Conservation Area which are not eligible under the Town Scheme.

TABLE FOUR
CONSERVATION FUND COMMITMENTS 1981/87

	1981/2	1982/3	1983/4	1984/5	1985/6	1986/7*
CITY TOWN SCHEME	117,435	113,444	106,494	118,147	104,064	60,000
CITY NON TOWN SCHEME	24,653	38,162	38,015	21,972	16,855	40,000
URBAN	8,254	10,648	7,082	15,999	22,969	23,000
RURAL	26,925	34,307	43,242	79,774	70,833	82,000

* The figures for 1986/87 represent the allocation for the year rather than the actual commitments.

TABLE FIVE
NUMBER OF HISTORIC BUILDINGS REQUIRING REPAIRS WITHIN FIVE YEARS

	MINIMUM OF £15,000 OF REPAIRS	MINIMUM OF £10,000 OF REPAIRS	MINIMUM OF £5,000 OF REPAIRS
CITY CENTRE	24	40	60
URBAN AREA	6	10	25
RURAL AREA	30	75	135

TABLE SIX
MINIMUM ANTICIPATED NEED FOR GRANT AID 1987/92

The figures in this Table are based on the minimum costs in table Four, and make no allowance for inflation over the five year period. It should also be noted that it is not possible to guarantee the timing of grant applications.

	COST OF ELIGIBLE REPAIRS	NORMAL GRANT	TOTAL GRANT AID (£)
CITY TOWN SCHEME*	600,000	15%	90,000
CITY NON TOWN SCHEME*	150,000	20%	30,000
URBAN	315,000	25%	78,750
RURAL	1,875,000	25%	468,750

* It has been assumed that 25% of buildings requiring repair in the City Conservation Area are owned by national companies and are therefore ineligible for grant aid.

Grants from this budget were exceptionally high in 1982/83 and 1983/84, principally because of allocations for the West Wing of Chester Station and the former Grosvenor Park Baptist Church. Apart from these, the level of grants has remained fairly constant. This budget is used for matching Section 10 grants from the Historic Buildings and Monuments Commission and for grants to important buildings on the fringe of the City Conservation Area.

The recent work in the Albion Street Housing Action Area has demonstrated the successful use of Section 10 grants linked to Housing Improvement grants, with a small number of grants from the Conservation Fund. With the completion of work in the Egerton Street Housing Action Area during 1987/88 it is anticipated that the need for grants in this category will reduce [see Tables Five and Six].

[c] URBAN BUDGET - to provide grants for buildings within the area of the Greater Chester Local Plan, excluding the City Conservation Area. Pressure for grants in this area has increased fairly steadily over the past five years. This reflects the need to extend the successful policies of the city centre into the immediately surrounding areas. Six priority problem buildings have been identified in the urban area [see G.3].

This budget includes the allocation for the Boughton Riverside Scheme, where the Council's grants are matched by Section 10 grants from the Historic Buildings and Monuments Commission. Applications for grants under this scheme are outstripping the present allocation and consideration should be given to increasing the budget and extending the life of the scheme. Apart from this special scheme, the present pressure for grant aid in this area is likely to be maintained.

[d] RURAL BUDGET — to provide grants for buildings within the area of the Chester Rural Area Local Plan. This budget has seen a very substantial increase in requests for grant aid over the past five years. This is likely to continue to increase, largely because the new List of Buildings of Special Architectural or Historic Interest contains four times as many buildings as the previous List for the rural area. The majority of rural listed buildings are small, but a significant proportion are timber framed and a number have thatched roofs. Repairs to these buildings tend to be very expensive and can involve a high level of grant aid. If the character of the rural area is to be maintained, these buildings will need grant aid to ensure their proper restoration.

The inspection of historic buildings in the rural area has identified nineteen priority problem buildings [see G.3] and a further 221 that require repair over the next five years. There is therefore likely to be an increasing need for grant aid from this budget in future years [see Tables Five and Six]. This will be particularly true if it proves possible to establish a number of special grant schemes for rural areas in conjunction with the County Council and the Historic Buildings and Monuments Commission [see E.2.1].

The Council's scheme of grants for historic buildings has been gradually refined over the past seventeen years. A comprehensive criteria for grants was approved in 1982, but minor amendments have been made since. An updated criteria is included at the end of this Review [see G.5]. This also proposes one further change; that the installation of damp proof courses should no longer be eligible for conservation grants. Damp proof courses are seldom essential to the well-being of buildings, normally being installed for the comfort of occupants.

Although grants from the Conservation Fund are the most obvious element of the City Council's financial contribution, they do not represent its full expenditure on conservation. For example, during 1984/85 over £600,000 was made available for conservation related matters, as shown in Table Seven. The majority of these items attracted government grant and two of them have been submitted for grant aid from the European Regional Development Fund.

Until recently the Council has been able to allocate a number of Home Improvement grants to conservation schemes. This proved a particularly effective way of assisting difficult schemes such as the reuse of upper floors. Consideration should be given to similar allocations in the future.

Unfortunately, the City Council's conservation responsibilities are not reflected in the Rate Support Grant. This is calculated using the Government's Grant Related Expenditure Assessment [GREA], which includes a factor under planning implementation purporting to relate to the 'Establishment of Conservation Areas'. However, this factor is distributed on the basis of population; therefore Chester receives no more allowance than any other District with a similar population.

This is one of the factors causing the Council's expenditure to exceed its GREA: with the result that, for 1986/87, it loses 60 pence in grant for every additional £1 it spends. With the volume of statistics available on listed buildings and other conservation expenditure it is to be regretted that the Department of the Environment will not introduce a more equitable basis for distributing this element of the Rate Support Grant.

ii County Council Finance

Cheshire County Council has a budget for grants to historic buildings, the majority of which is taken up with Town Scheme commitments outside the Chester district. The remainder is available as small grants for the repair of Grade I and II* buildings, and for Grade II buildings in conservation areas. They also operate a small Conservation Action Fund which is geared to help special cases not necessarily related to listed buildings. The City and County grant policies do not complement each other and this sometimes leads to

TABLE SEVEN
CONSERVATION RELATED BUDGETS 1984/85   £

CONSERVATION FUND (INCLUDING INTEREST)	196,500
THE GROVES IMPROVEMENT — PHASE ONE	70,000
PEDESTRIANISATION — PHASE THREE	70,000
REPAIRS TO COUNCIL-OWNED HISTORIC BUILDINGS	75,000
REPAIRS TO CITY WALLS	35,000
ACQUISITION OF ROCK FARM, ELTON	27,500
STAFF SALARIES AND OVERHEADS	152,740
TOTAL	626,740

apparently arbitary discrepancies between similar buildings within the district.

The County Council also has a budget for rural conservation, tree planting and ecology; and negotiates and administers a substantial Countryside Commission grant scheme.

iii Grants from Historic Buildings and Monuments Commission

In April 1984 the Historic Buildings and Monuments Commission for England [English Heritage] took over most of the work concerning historic buildings and ancient monuments previously undertaken by the Historic Buildings Council and the Department of the Environment.

The Council's Conservation Programme has been fully supported by the Historic Buildings Council and the Department of the Environment; and now by the Commission. Very substantial financial resources have been made available, much advice has been given, and without their encouragement in resolving difficulties many of the restoration schemes now completed would never have started.

The Commission make grants available in five main categories:

1. Repairs to Ancient Monuments.
2. Repairs to Outstanding Secular Buildings.
3. Repairs to Outstanding Churches.
4. Joint Funding of Town Schemes with Local Authorities.
5. Section 10 grants for the Enhancement of Conservation Areas.

The Town Scheme and Section 10 grants concentrate resources upon towns and some larger villages. As the Council's emphasis has shifted towards conservation outside the city centre, the assistance of the Commission has reduced. It is therefore proposed that the Council should not seek to renew its Section 10 Programme status with the Commission for 1987/88 and subsequent years. This will mean that requests for Section 10 grants will be considered in the light of the general funds available for all applications from the region.

The Council have been very concerned at the Commission's increasing restrictions on eligibility for their grants, as a method of stretching its limited budget. Most recently, the strong presumption against a grant for anyone who has purchased a building within the past four years, and the refusal to consider an increase of grant for the first 10% increase in costs, has made the work of encouraging the repair of historic buildings much more difficult. In the City Council's view these measures significantly reduce the scope and effectiveness of the Commission's grant schemes.

iv Other Sources of Finance

The Chester Historic Buildings Preservation Trust was established in 1981, but it has been unable to find a suitable building within the city centre, for its first project. In 1985 it decided to consider buildings in the rural area and is at present planning to purchase No. 3 Church Cottages, Tarvin, from the Council. The Trust would operate on the principle of a revolving fund, raising money through donations, grants and a loan from the Architectural Heritage Fund.

A number of private trusts can make grants for the restoration of historic buildings, although they generally prefer to support other trusts or charitable groups rather than private individuals or companies. The Pilgrim Trust, for example, contributed to the restoration of the Falcon, Lower Bridge Street, by the Falcon Trust.

Initiatives connected with tourism may be eligible for grants from the English Tourist Board and the European Regional Development Fund. The EEC also makes annual grants for the preservation of buildings and monuments of national significance. As the emphasis of the Conservation Programme moves towards the rural areas, the Council will become more closely concerned with the Countryside Commission, the Forestry Commission, the Development Commission and the Ministry of Agriculture and Fisheries, all of whom make money available for a variety of work in the countryside.

E.3.2.
PEOPLE

Major repair projects are normally carried out under the direction of architects, engineers or surveyors. Smaller schemes generally only involve the owner and builder. In both situations, but particularly in the latter, there is a need for specialist understanding of sympathetic repair techniques [see D.3.9]. Specialist knowledge and understanding is also needed on the wider conservation front.

i. Conservation Consultancy

Recognition by the Council of the need for specialist involvement in conservation work goes back to 1971 when the Council, jointly with the Department of the Environment, engaged Donald W Insall and Associates as consultants. Initially they had responsibility for the Bridgegate Action Area, but later assisted with the production of the whole Conservation Programme. The consultants have carried out area surveys and produced feasibility studies at times when these activities were beyond the resources of the Council; and they have contributed their specialist expertise on a wide range of problems. The benefits of this arrangement have been substantial, but in the view of the Director of Technical Services, the most important results of the consultancy are less tangible. The good working relationship with the Department of the Environment and recently the Historic Buildings and Monuments Commission, the establishment of national and international links and the provision of an objective overview of the whole Programme, are substantially Donald Insall's achievement.

Since 1975, the involvement of the consultants has been progressively reduced and it was recognised in 1985 that, despite their valuable contribution, it could not be justified indefinitely. The Council has agreed with the Historic Buildings and Monuments Commission that the arrangements would be concluded in March 1987, following the preparation of this Review.

REPAIRS TO THE VICTORIAN CONSERVATORY AT HOOLE HALL
RECEIVED SUBSTANTIAL GRANT AID FROM THE URBAN BUDGET
IN 1987.

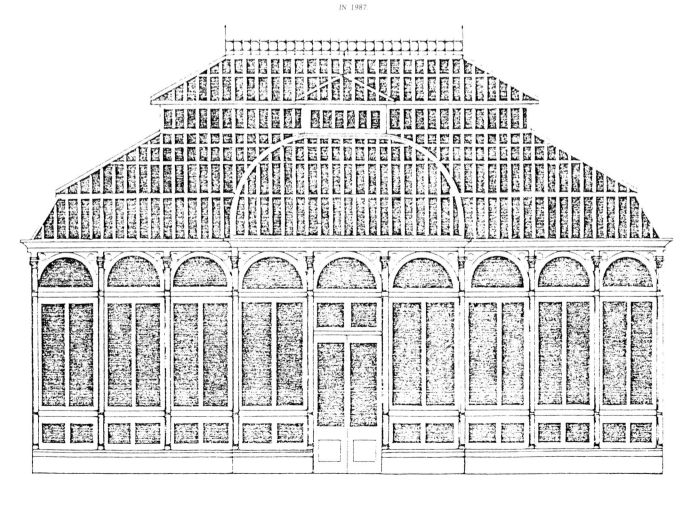

A CONSERVATION PROGRESS MEETING WITH (FROM LEFT TO RIGHT)
CYRIL MORRIS (DIRECTOR OF TECHNICAL SERVICES), ANDREW BROWN (CONSERVATION
OFFICER), DONALD INSALL (CONSERVATION CONSULTANT), ANNA McPHERSON
(HISTORIC BUILDINGS AND MONUMENTS COMMISSION)
AND CHRIS HARDY (PRINCIPAL PLANNING OFFICER).

ii City Council

In 1971 the Council appointed a Conservation Officer, whose principal role was to promote the recommendations contained in the 1968 Insall Report. Since then, the increasing range of activities has necessitated additional staff. In building up the Conservation Section, considerable care has been taken to ensure that its members have the practical expertise necessary to promote an active conservation programme. In Chester, little time has been spent in theorising about conservation - action takes precedence.

The Council's Conservation Section consists of the Conservation Officer, who is an architect, a Planning Assistant and three Conservation Assistants, together with clerical support. Also the Heritage Centre Assistant is seconded to the team for 50% of the time. This level of establishment is appropriate for the present workload, but the section may not have the necessary skills or manpower to support the increasing involvement in environmental improvements and tourism. Although the finance available for historic buildings may reduce, it is likely that smaller grants will be given to more buildings and therefore the administrative and supervisory workload will remain constant.

The Conservation Section is located within the Planning Division of the Department of Technical Services. Although the section is concerned with the day to day administration of the Conservation Programme, it works closely with the rest of the department. Conservation is an integral element in the control of the changing environment, and the present daily liaison with the Development Control Section is particularly important. There is also considerable involvement with, and specialist advice from, members of other departments.

The archaeological staff of the Grosvenor Museum make an important contribution to the Conservation Programme. Over recent years the links between the two sections have strengthened, particularly following the designation of the Area of Archaeological Importance. To plan and carry out an effective programme of investigation and rescue archaeology, areas of future change need to be identified and activities co-ordinated.

iii County Council

Cheshire County Council's Conservation Group provides expertise in four areas; historic buildings, archaeology, landscape and ecology. Their thorough work on the resurvey of the rural area for a new List of Buildings of Special Architectural or Historic Interest has been very useful and their specialist knowledge of historic buildings and archaeology provides an invaluable complement to that of the City Council's staff.

The City Council employs the County Council's landscape architects as consultants for the pedestrianisation paving programme and relies upon the County's staff for specialist advice on trees and landscape. This expertise, together with ecology, is likely to become of increasing importance to the Conservation Programme as the emphasis shifts towards the problems of historic rural areas.

iv Historic Buildings and Monuments
Commission

The staff of the Historic Buildings and Monuments Commission provide advice and expertise over a wide range of matters connected with the conservation of buildings and monuments. The Council benefits particularly from their knowledge of architectural history and their technical expertise in difficult restoration work. Possibly of greater value, however, is the fact that they have experience of conservation nationally; being able to advise on the relative importance of buildings or problems and provide links to other authorities with similar problems, but different solutions.

v Major Owners

The Eaton Estate, home of the Duke of Westminster, owns 153 structures included on the List of Buildings of Special Architectural or Historic Interest. This represents almost 10% of the listed buildings in the district. The majority of these are on the Eaton country estate, centred around Eaton Park, which is itself included on the Register of Parks and Gardens of Special Historic Interest. The Estate is generally to be applauded for its care of the environment, and in particular for the recent adoption of a landscape conservation plan.

Although the Eaton Estate is an extreme example, significant groups of listed buildings and substantial areas of landscape are in other single ownerships, a number of whom also have a developing interest in tourism and leisure. There are obvious advantages in establishing good working relationships with such major owners, who range from traditional country estates to companies such as the British Shoe Corporation. While some have appreciated the advantages of working closely with the Council, others are suspicious, doubtful or hostile. The work that has been undertaken by the Dean and Chapter of the Cathedral [see C.2.0] and by the Shotwick Estate [see C.11.2] has demonstrated the benefits of good co-operation.

The main problem common to virtually all these major owners is that their buildings and landscapes have been badly maintained in the past, and they face major expenditure if these historic features are to be retained. Even with the benefit of grants, the majority of the finance has still to be found by the owners. There are a significant number who are unwilling or unable to make this level of financial commitment, often seeing conservation as an unrealistic interference in their business. It is therefore important for the Council to understand their aims and intentions, and to enter into a genuine dialogue on future possibilities. The alternative is constant irritation and misunderstanding on both sides, with threats of time consuming legal action by the Council.

vi Public Support

The Conservation Programme has received the staunch support of the public [see D.1.3]. This creates an atmosphere which encourages owners and developers to repair and conserve, rather than to neglect and redevelop. The general public also act as the ears and eyes of the Conservation Team; they notice when things change and bring them to the attention of the Council. In some cases the Council may already be aware of the activity, but in many others this early warning system is invaluable.

Since 1970 the Council have had the benefit of advice from a Conservation Area Advisory Committee, which co-ordinates the views of eleven groups with an interest in the environment of the city centre. Their major influence so far has been through consultation and comments on planning applications. As the opportunities for major development in the City Centre Conservation Area reduce it may be appropriate for the Committee to review their role, possibly developing their increasing interest in initiating enhancement schemes.

E.3.3.
Legal Powers

The whole basis of the Council's Conservation Programme rests on the concept of listed buildings and conservation areas enshrined in the Town and Country Planning Act 1971, and associated legislation. Generally these legal powers are

appropriate for the protection of the historic environment; and although there are some people who would wish the local planning authority to have greater powers, others think there should be less control. Thus the balance is probably correct.

Chester District has some 1,635 listed buildings and 40 conservation areas. The new List of Buildings of Special Architectural or Historic Interest for the rural area is both comprehensive and up-to-date. The List for the city centre and the inner suburban areas is proving increasingly inadequate, mainly because of changes in listing policy since it was completed in 1972. This list is particulary weak in the following ways:

1. It under-estimates the importance of many of the Rows buildings because of a lack of internal investigation.
2. There is inadequate coverage of the industrial structures associated with the canal and the river.
3. Limited coverage of nineteenth century buildings, chiefly in the following suburbs; Boughton, Curzon Park; Dee Banks, Handbridge, Hoole, Hough Green and Queens Park.
4. No coverage of the nineteenth century cemeteries.
5. Omission of significant late nineteenth century and early twentieth century buildings, particularly those that continue the Chester 'black and white' tradition.

The 1976 Review Study included a schedule of buildings for submission to the Department of the Environment as being eligible for the List of Buildings of Special Architectural and Historic Interest. None of these suggestions have yet been added to the list. Rather than suggest specific buildings for listing in this study, it is recommended that the Department of the Environment be requested to arrange an urgent resurvey of the city centre and the inner suburban areas. This could be carried out by the County Council, in the same way as its staff acted as delegated inspectors for the resurvey of the rural area.

The majority of the conservation areas recommended in the two 1976 Review Studies have now been designated. There appears limited opportunity for further conservation areas in the suburban area or the villages, but it may be appropriate to consider the designation of a small number of historic rural landscapes, such as Edge, near Malpas.

The Council make full use of the legal powers available for conservation, particularly the Listed Building Consent procedures under Section 55 of the Town and Country Planning Act 1971, and Repairs Notices, under Section 115 of the same Act. Various discrepancies in the present legislative framework act against effective conservation. The strange division between Scheduled Monuments and Listed Buildings, the extended consultation procedures that prevent rapid decisions and the lack of any clear definition of 'demolition' or 'partial demolition' all create problems; but the most insidious discrepancy remains the imposition of VAT on repairs to historic buildings. However, the two areas of legislative weakness that have particularly frustrated the Council are the lack of powers to preserve unlisted buildings and the cumbersome enforcement procedures. In considering future legislation, these should be urgently reviewed by the Department of the Environment.

[i] Preservation of unlisted buildings in conservation areas

Section 101 of the Town and Country Planning Act 1971, as amended, gives a local authority powers to carry out work necessary for the preservation of unoccupied buildings in conservation areas. This power has proved to be of limited use. The main problem is that it cannot be applied to a building which is partially occupied, even if the unoccupied section is being allowed to deteriorate. Similarly, there is no action that can be taken to save an occupied building which is deteriorating. A further limitation is that the works have to be the minimum necessary. This means that if the owner is determined to continue neglecting the buildings, the legislation has

to be invoked year after year to ensure continued preservation of the building.

[ii] Enforcement Action

The character of a historic area relies not only on the general composition of buildings, spaces and landscape, but on the details of the many individual elements. It is these details which are most at risk and which are easily lost, leading to a steady erosion of historic character.

To prevent the loss of these details requires effective enforcement action, but the present procedures are cumbersome and time consuming. This means that their use can seldom be justified for the protection of small items, such as doors, glazing bars, patterned slating or decorative rainwater goods; or for the removal of minor but damaging additions, signs, blinds or ventilation grilles. Not only does this mean that details are not reinstated, it leads to a casual attitude from owners and developers, who know that the Council are unlikely to take any action against minor losses and infringements.

TYPICAL EATON ESTATE COTTAGES.

133

THE SPUR WALL LINKING THE WATER TOWER TO THE CITY WALLS.

F

THE CONTINUING PROGRAMME

Chester is not a museum piece to be preserved without alteration.... new times bring

new needs.

W Matthews Jones,
Mayor of Chester,
Greenwood Report,
1945

F

THE CONTINUING PROGRAMME

THIS FURTHER REVIEW STUDY has been a valuable exercise. By analysing past activities and assessing the continuing problems within a changing development framework, it becomes possible to recommend ways in which the Conservation Programme can go forward for the next ten years.

The conservation and enhancement of the District's heritage and environment are major factors in the city's success as a service and tourist centre. Chester's economic life relies heavily on this image; and the contribution of the Conservation Programme in caring for the environment of both the city and the surrounding area cannot be over-estimated. In view of the importance of the District's image, it is recommended that the Conservation Programme should continue, and that it should be complimented by an Environmental Improvement Programme and a Tourist Strategy. This will ensure the continued preservation and enhancement of the district; helping with economic development and providing a framework for the fuller use of the historic qualities of the area.

For the purpose of this Review and the following recommendations it has been assumed that the aims of the Council's current planning policies, as detailed in the Local Plans, will remain broadly constant for the next ten years.

THE ARCHITECTURAL VARIETY OF BRIDGE STREET.

F.1.0
RESOURCES

We recommend the following objectives and actions:

F.1.1   Continue to review the Conservation Fund on a three year basis, rolled forward each year, assessing the likely level of finance required for three years hence at any particular time (see E.3.1.i.).

F.1.2   Contribute the product of at least three-quarters of a penny rate to the Conservation Fund for the three years 1987/90.

This would amount to approximately £140,000 per annum; a reduction from the present contribution of a penny rate (£184,000 in 1986/87) and even with the expected interest of £20,000 is less than the minimum anticipated need for grant aid (see Table Six, E.3.1.i). However, it is impossible to guarantee the timing of grant applications and it is unlikely that all the identified repairs will be carried out within a five year period. The Conservation Fund currently holds an unallocated balance of approximately £35,000, being monies returned to the Fund. A three-quarters penny rate, together with this balance, would allow for the budget recommendations indicated in Table Eight.

F.1.3   Continue the present Council Scheme of Grants on the basis of the revised criteria (see E.3.1.i and G.5).

F.1.4   The Chester Town Scheme of Grants, operated jointly by the Council and the Historic Buildings and Monuments Commission, having largely fulfilled its aim of encouraging the repair of historic buildings within the city centre, could be terminated at the end of the present three year agreement in March 1989 (see E.3.1.i).

F.1.5   The success of the Conservation Programme in the city centre has reduced the need for a Section 10 Programme Allocation from the Historic Buildings and Monuments Commission and therefore from 1987/88 applications will only be made for individual projects (see E.3.1.iii).

F.1.6   Request the Historic Buildings and Monuments Commission to consider an increase in the annual allocation for the Boughton Riverside Section 10 Scheme from £5,000 to £6,000 and to extend the scheme until 1989/90 (see E.2.1 and E.3.1.i).

F.1.7   Hold further discussions with the Historic Buildings and Monuments Commission and other bodies on methods of financing the conservation of historic rural areas (see D.3.6).

F.1.8   Hold further discussions with the County Council in order to make more effective concerted use of the grants available from both authorities (see E.3.1.ii).

F.1.9   Continue to maintain Capital and Revenue Budgets for a programme of repairs to the City Walls (see C.7.0).

F.1.10   Provision to be made within the Conservation Fund for a small budget to provide interpretative plaques for the historic monuments and buildings of the district (see E.2.4).

CONSERVATION FUND BUDGET RECOMMENDATIONS 1987/92

The figures in this table make no allowance for inflation over the five year period.

The allocations shown for the City budgets are higher than the anticipated need in Table Six because of the likelihood of grant being required for upper floor schemes after the end of the Town Scheme.

	1987/88	1988/89	1989/90	1990/91	1991/92
CITY TOWN SCHEME	60,000	60,000	—	—	—
CITY NON TOWN SCHEME	10,000	10,000	30,000	30,000	30,000
URBAN	15,000	15,000	15,000	15,000	15,000
BOUGHTON RIVERSIDE	6,000	6,000	6,000	—	—
RURAL	80,000	80,000	80,000	80,000	80,000
FIRST AID	2,000	2,000	2,000	2,000	2,000
DEBT CHARGES ON ACQUISITIONS	2,000	2,000	2,000	2,000	2,000
INTERPRETATIVE PLAQUES	1,000	1,000	1,000	1,000	1,000
TOTALS	176,000	176,000	136,000	130,000	130,000

F.1.11 Provision to be made in the Council's Capital Programme for the following enhancement proposals:-

(a) Extension of the programme of pedestrian paving into Bridge Street and Watergate Street (see E.2.3).

(b) Extension of the improvements to The Groves as far as the Old Dee Bridge (see C.8.0 and E.2.3).

(c) An Improvement Programme for Small Sites (see E.2.3)

(d) A Landscape Improvement Programme (see E.2.2).

(e) A Conservation Areas Enhancement Programme (see E.2.3).

F.1.12 Each year make six Home Improvement Grants available for allocation to conservation schemes (see E.3.1.i).

F.1.13 Continue to monitor the total amount of grant aid given to churches, to ensure that they do not receive too high a proportion of the Conservation Fund (see D.3.5).

F.1.14 Support the efforts of the Chester Historic Buildings Preservation Trust to establish a revolving fund (see E.3.1.iv).

F.1.15 Maintain the Council's links with the Historic Buildings and Monuments Commission at all levels (see E.3.2.iv).

F.1.16 Improve liaison between the Conservation Section of the Department of Technical Services, the archaeological staff of the Grosvenor Museum, the Heritage Centre and the City Record Office, particularly in developing the tourist potential of the District's heritage (see E.2.4 and E.3.2.i).

F.1.17 Invite the Conservation Area Advisory Committee to reconsider its role, possibly to provide initiative and support for the general improvement of the environment (see E.3.2.vi).

F.1.18 Review the Council's requirement for specialist advice on trees and landscape, in the light of developing programmes of rural conservation and enhancement.

F.1.19 Request the Department of the Environment to arrange the early resurvey of the city centre and the inner urban areas with a view to revising the List of Buildings of Special Architectural or Historic Interest (E.3.3).

F.1.20 Request the Department of the Environment to consider ways of increasing the powers of local planning authorities to protect unlisted buildings in conservation areas, particularly when amendments to legislation are planned (see E.3.3).

F.1.21 Request the Department of the Environment to consider ways of improving the present arrangements for enforcement action, particularly when amendments to legislation are planned (see E.3.3).

F.2.0
MAINTAINING PROGRESS

We recommend the following objectives and actions:

F.2.1   Continue to hold regular meetings, chaired by the Director of Technical Services, to review and guide the progress of the Conservation Programme; and the Historic Buildings and Monuments Commission be invited to send a representative to these meetings (see B).

F.2.2   Inspect the condition of all historic buildings every five years, to identify developing problems and determine the future need for grant aid (see B, D.2.2 and D.3.1).

F.2.3   Take action to ensure the repair of the forty-five priority problem buildings identified (see D.3.1 and G.3).

F.2.4   Investigate means of ensuring the repair of the six structures of limited economic use identified as priorities (see D.3.2 and G.4).

F.2.5   Give encouragement to schemes to bring back into full use the properties identified as having vacant or underused upper floors (see C.2, D.3.3 and G.3).

F.2.6   Continue the programme of Conservation Area Studies (see E.2.0).

F.2.7   Support and encourage a positive contribution from all groups, bodies and individuals engaged in the care of the District's heritage (see E.3.2).

F.2.8   Maintain links with other historic towns in Britain and Europe, particularly through Europa Nostra (see B).

F.2.9   Update the agreement with the County Council on the materials to be used for the repair of pavements in the city centre (see B).

F.2.10   Monitor the movement of key sections of the City Walls in order to give advance notice of developing problems (see C.7.0).

F.2.11   Continue the present policies adopted for Brook Street, refusing applications to alter or remove unspoilt Victorian shopfronts, carefully controlling advertisements and offering grant aid where appropriate (see C.10.0).

F.2.12   Continue to support the Section 10 Scheme for Shotwick Conservation Area, and encourage the repair of the ancillary buildings which make a substantial contribution to the character of the village (see C.11.2).

F.3.0
INITIATIVES

We recommend the following objectives and action:

F.3.1   Designate a conservation area at Edge, near Malpas, and hold further discussions with the Historic Buildings and Monuments Commission and other bodies on the possibilities of using Edge as a pilot project for the conservation of historic rural areas (see D.3.6).

F.3.2   Research the possibility of establishing a 'Conservation Workshop', in conjunction with the Manpower Services Commission, Cheshire County Council, the Dean and Chapter of the Cathedral and the Chester Diocesan Board, so as to provide practical training in conservation skills at all levels (see D.3.9).

F.3.3   Identify areas in need of additional grant aid and explore the possibility of establishing special schemes, in conjunction with Cheshire County Council, the Historic Buildings and Monuments Commission and other bodies (see E.2.1).

F.3.4   Investigate alternative methods of achieving the restoration of structures of limited economic use; such as increased grant aid, sponsorship and MSC schemes or as part of a training programme (see D.3.2).

F.3.5   Investigate the possibility of the City Council taking over responsibility for the lighting on the City Walls, on an agency basis from the County Council (see C.7.0).

F.3.6   Consider the introduction of more imaginative lighting arrangements for the Rows (see C.1.0).

F.3.7   Discuss alternative methods of traffic management with the County Council, the Cheshire Constabulary and the Department of Transport, and investigate whether Chester could experiment with different solutions (see D.3.4).

F.3.8   Investigate the possibility of establishing residents' parking schemes, particularly in King Street and Albion Street (see C.3.0 and C.6.0).

F.3.9   Monitor the use of gardens and yards for car parking and take appropriate action to improve the appearance of these areas (see D.3.4).

F.3.10 Seek to ensure the adequate recording of all historic buildings before and during major restoration schemes, possibly in conjunction with the Rows Survey Project, the Grosvenor Museum or the County Council (see D.2.4).

F.3.11 Initiate the preparation of interpretative material and plaques on the origins and development of the City Walls, the Rows and other major buildings (see E.2.4).

F.3.12 Promote the following conservation projects:

(a)   Extend the principles of the Nicholas Street restoration scheme into adjacent areas, such as Lower Watergate Street and Stanley Place (see C.4.0).

(b)   Encourage the repair and renovation of Nos 16-18 and Nos 26-36 Seller Street, to maintain and improve the existing character (see C.10.0).

(c)   Investigate the introduction of a one way street system in the King Street area (see C.3.0).

(d)   Continue negotiations to facilitate the residential development of land to the north of Rock Farm, Elton (see C.11.3).

REPAIRS IN PROGRESS IN WATERGATE STREET.

F.4.0

DEVELOPMENT OPPORTUNITIES

We recommend the following objectives and action:

F.4.1   Promote the improvement of Eastgate Street Row North and Bridge Street Row West as small scale shopping areas (see C.1.0 and E.1.1).

F.4.2   Encourage the continuing development of further small scale pedestrian shopping areas behind the main Rows frontages, similar to Godstall Lane (see C.1.0, D.3.3 and E.1.1).

F.4.3   Fully support the excavation of the southern part of the Roman amphitheatre and the development of appropriate interpretative facilities (see C.8.0 and E.2.4).

F.4.4   Fully support the improvement of the Inner Ward of the Castle as a major tourist attraction (see E.2.4).

F.4.5   Explore the possibility of displaying the Roman buildings in Abbey Green (see C.2.0).

F.4.6   Sell the Weaver Street car park for appropriate development as soon as possible, to improve the appearance of this prominent site.

F.4.7   Encourage appropriate developments along the Inner Ring Road between the Northgate roundabout and The Bars, to improve the appearance of the area (see C.9.0).

F.4.8   Encourage the development of the following sites, in order to improve the appearance of the City Conservation Area and to support other Council policies:

(a)   The site to the rear of Nos 5 and 6 Kings Buildings
(b)   The garage on the west side of Nicholas Street Mews
(c)   The gap site on the east side of Lower Bridge Street
(d)   The site on the north side of Albion Street.
(e)   The site at the north-east end of Foregate Street, adjacent to No 117.
(f)   The site of the former Methodist Central Hall, City Road.
(g)   The small site south of No 33 City Road.
(h)   The Royalty Theatre, City Road, and the garage to the south, preferably retaining the theatre auditorium.
(j)   The Angel site at the junction of Egerton Street and Brook Street.
(k)   Tower Wharf.

F.5.0

ENVIRONMENTAL IMPROVEMENTS

We recommend the following objectives and action:

F.5.1   Continue the programme of pedestrian paving into Bridge Street and Watergate Street (see E.2.3).

F.5.2   Extend the improvements of the Riverside as far as the Old Dee Bridge (see C.8.0 and E.2.3).

F.5.3   Support the Conservation Area Advisory Committee in their wish to see substantial improvements to City Road and the Station Forecourt (see C.10.0).

F.5.4   Extend the King Street surfacing scheme to the area in front of Kings Buildings and investigate the possibility of planting some trees in this area (see C.3.0).

F.5.5   Complete the Albion Street scheme by reinstating a traditional road surface (see C.6.0).

F.5.6   Investigate the possibility of improving the pavement surfaces and street furniture throughout the Bridgegate Area (see C.5.0).

F.5.7   Encourage the Dean and Chapter to initiate the following improvements:

(a)   Repair of the surface of Abbey Green (see C.2.0).

(b)   Reinstatement of the railings to the grassed area in the centre of Abbey Square (see C.2.0).

F.5.8   Investigate ways of improving the setting of the City Walls, particularly to the south of the Castle and between the Eastgate and Newgate (see C.7.0).

F.5.9   Initiate proposals to uncover the historic street surfaces in minor streets, such as Bunce Street, Castle Street and Whitefriars (see E.2.3).

F.6.0
CONTROL POLICIES

We recommend the following objectives and action:

F.6.1   Encourage a high standard of sympathetic modern design for new developments in conservation areas (see D.3.8).

F.6.2   Seek additional planning control, through Article 4 Directions, in residential areas that are vulnerable to the unsympathetic alteration of architectural details (see D.3.8).

F.6.3   Establish a presumption against the conversion of listed farmbuildings for residential use, prefering office or light industrial uses subject to other planning considerations (see D.3.7).

F.6.4   Resist the erection of railings, separating the Row walkways from the stalls and make every effort to encourage the removal of the existing railings in these positions (see C.1.0).

F.6.5   Seek to maintain the use of traditional materials for the Rows walkways and stalls (see C.1.0).

F.6.6   Accept that the only way to maintain many of the large Victorian houses in the urban conservation areas is to allow sympathetic sub-division (see C.11.0).

F.6.7   Resist the development of new houses in the gardens and other open spaces of the urban conservation areas (see C.11.0).

F.7.0
FUTURE REVIEW

We recommend that:

F.7.1   A further decennial review of the Conservation programme be carried out in 1996.

EIGHTEENTH CENTURY HOUSES ON SOUTH SIDE OF STANLEY PLACE.

LOOKING ACROSS EASTGATE STREET FROM THE ROWS.

APPENDICES

The life of a local authority conservation officer is not easy.

He must have the eye of an eagle, the persuasive tongue of a Demosthenes, and the

diplomatic skills of a Bismarck or a Kissinger.

Especially when dealing with inscrutable orientals. Take Roger Tilley city conservation

officer of Chester. He had to go round to a Chinese resturant

in Watergate Street to try to persuade the proprietor, a Mr Ng, to remove vertical

pictograms from his premises' historic Rows facade. Could he not,

asked Tilley, run his name sign HORIZONTALLY like everyone else in the Rows.

At this Mr. Ng became quite excited. 'Chinese lighting goes unk'

[swift downward stroke of palm], 'not unk!' [horizontal karate chop narrowly missing

conservation officer's head]. Retreat of Tilley in some confusion.

Whatever the merits or demerits of his vertical lettering, however,

Chester conservationists are generally agreed that Mr Ng's cuisine

is very good indeed.

Scorpio,
Building Design.

G

APPENDICES

G.1
CONSERVATION AWARDS TO THE CITY COUNCIL

1971
The Royal Institution of Chartered Surveyors - The Times Conservation Award
The Nine Houses, Park Street

1975
Civic Trust Award for Exceptional Merit, European Architectural Heritage Year
Conservation in Chester

Civic Trust European Architectural Heritage Year Awards
Gamul House and Cottages in Gamul Place and Gamul Terrace, Lower Bridge Street
No 51 Watergate Street
The Dutch Houses, Bridge Street

British Tourist Authority Commendation
Heritage Centre

1978
Civic Trust Commendation
St Peter's Churchyard

1981
European Prize for the Preservation of Historical Monuments
Conservation in Chester

1983
Europa Nostra Award
Bridgegate Conservation Action Area

1985
The Royal Town Planning Institute Commendation for Planning Achievement
Conservation in Chester

1986
Civic Trust Award
Pedestrianisation: The Cross, Eastgate Street and Northgate Street

CONSERVATION AREAS

Date of Designation

Chester City . . . . January 1969
    Egerton Street Extension . . . . July 1980
    Canal Basin Extension . . . . April 1981
    *City Road/Brook St Extension . November 1984

Malpas . . . . December 1969
    Extended . . . . March 1981
Tattenhall . . . . July 1970
    Extended . . . . October 1985
Farndon . . . . November 1972
Tarvin . . . . February 1973
Christleton . . . . March 1973
Aldersey Green . . . . July 1973
Barton . . . . July 1973
Burton . . . . July 1973
Churton . . . . July 1973
Coddington . . . . July 1973
Handley . . . . July 1973
Harthill . . . . July 1973
Tilston . . . . July 1973
Tiverton . . . . July 1973
Shotwick . . . . February 1974
Aldford . . . . March 1974

Flookersbrook . . . . November 1976
Great Barrow . . . . March 1979
Ashton . . . . April 1979
Dunham . . . . April 1979
Ledsham . . . . April 1979
Stoak . . . . April 1979
Waverton . . . . April 1979
Elton . . . . April 1979
Handbridge . . . . April 1979
Curzon Park . . . . April 1979
Queens Park . . . . August 1979
Eccleston . . . . August 1979
Boughton and The Meadows . . . . October 1979
Bruera . . . . October 1979
Saighton . . . . October 1979
Little Barrow . . . . January 1980
Beeston . . . . January 1980
Kelsall . . . . March 1980
*Chester Station . . . . April 1980
Sheaf . . . . April 1980
Puddington . . . . July 1980
Clotton . . . . November 1980
Thornton le Moors . . . . October 1981
Saughall . . . . June 1982

*The City Road/Brook Street Extension to the Chester City Conservation Area absorbed the
Chester Station Conservation Area.

G.3.
PRIORITY PROBLEM BUILDINGS

This list includes buildings considered to require urgent repairs costing at least £15,000 in November 1986

City Conservation Area
1 Abbey Green
17 and 19 Bridge Street Row [Upper Floor]
45a, 45b and 47a Bridge Street Row
63 and 65 Bridge Street Row [Upper Floor]
71 and 73 Bridge Street Row [Upper Floor]
6 Eastgate Street Row [Upper Floor]
8 and 10 Eastgate Street Row [Upper Floor]
57 Egerton Street
59, 61, 63 and 65 Egerton Street and
2 Leadworks Lane
The Old Palace, The Groves
15 Lower Bridge Street [Upper Floor]
18 Nicholas Street
100 Northgate Street
1 and 3 Nuns Road
16, 16a and 18 Seller Street
30, 32 and 34 Seller Street
St Barnabas' Church, Sibell Street
East Wing, Chester Station, Station Road
59 Watergate Street Row
1 Whitefriars

Urban Area
119 and 121 Boughton
St Paul's Church, Boughton
7 Lower Park Road
Newton Hall, Plas Newton Lane
18, 20 and 22 Tarvin Road
Farmbuildings, Wrexham Road Farm

Rural Area
Brook Farm Cottage, Beeston
Barn, Brassey Green Hall
Broxton Lower Hall
Keeper's Cottage, Carden
Brook Cottage, Clotton Hoofield
Clutton Lodges, Clutton
3 The Bank, Edge
Brassey's Contract Cottage, Edge
Park Cottages, Edge
Mickerdale Cottage, Harthill
Peel Hall, Horton cum Peel
Shippon, Moor End Farm, Kinnerton
Tudor Cottage, Old Hall Street, Malpas
3 Church Cottages, Tarvin
51 High Street Tarvin

Roade House, 55 High Street, Tarvin
86 High Street, Tarvin
Poolbank Cottage, Tarvin
Trafford Hall, Wimbolds Trafford

G.4
STRUCTURES AT RISK
This list includes structures of limited economic use which required urgent repairs in November 1986.

Walled Garden, Aldersey Hall, Aldersey
Walled Garden, Churton Hall, Churton
Ice House, Mollington Hall, Mollington
Derelict Building, Whitchurch Road, Rowton
Windmill, Threapwood
Tilstone Hall Folly, Tilstone Fearnall

G.5
CRITERIA FOR GRANT AID TO HISTORIC BUILDINGS IN CHESTER

The present policy of the City Council is, as far as possible, to secure grant aid for every historic building where eligible repairs are proposed. To that end, the Council operates its own scheme of grant aid and also co-operates with the Historic Buildings and Monument Commission through Town Schemes and Section 10 grant schemes. The Commission also make separate grants for 'outstanding' buildings.

The Local Authorities [Historic Buildings] Act 1962, which enables the Council to give grant aid for the repair or maintenance of historic buildings, acknowledged the considerable burden which has been placed on the private owners of listed and other important historic buildings. A key factor is the disproportionately high cost of proper repairs to historic fabric, as compared with the cost of economic or utility repairs likely to be very damaging to their character. Many local Planning Authorities recognise the importance of the conservation of old buildings and have made funds available for grant aid.

In Chester there has long been an appreciation that 'the face of the City is its fortune', and there is a very deep commitment not only to retain the best of its architectural heritage but also to ensure the highest quality of new development.

Since the inception of the City Council's Conservation Fund in 1970, the grant policies and procedures have been continuously updated and refined and now represent one of the most effective and flexible systems in the country. The availability of grant aid is, of course, only one part of the complex process of conservation management. However, it is a fundamental part; without which the essential process of building repair and regeneration becomes infinitely more difficult to achieve.

The owner of any listed building within the Chester District has an expectation of grant aid for eligible repairs to the property, subject to funds being available at the time of application. This document defines the general attitudes which govern the Council's grants, but the rules may vary slightly, especially in schemes which are operated in conjunction with the Historic Buildings and Monuments Commission.

BUILDINGS ELIGIBLE FOR GRANT

Disregarding any assessment of priority which may be placed on a building because of its state of deterioration, the criterion used in considering a building for grant must be its architectural or historic merit. The view is usually taken that the more important a building the greater the level of grant aid which should be available for its repair. Grants are usually offered for repairs to buildings in one of the following categories:

(a) Scheduled Ancient Monuments
(b) Buildings on the List of Buildings of Special Architectural or Historic Interest.
(c) Key historic buildings in conservation areas.
(d) Buildings that contribute to the character of conservation areas.
(e) Any other building of architectural or historic interest which makes a significant contribution to the environment.

The level of grant is related to the importance of the building, and to the rules of the particular grant scheme. In addition to the schemes operated by the City Council and the Historic Buildings

TABLE NINE
GUIDELINES FOR GRANTS TO HISTORIC BUILDINGS IN CHESTER

	CITY COUNCIL	COUNTY† COUNCIL	HBMC	NORMAL MAXIMUM
TOWN SCHEME (CITY CONS. AREA ONLY)	15%	—	15%	30%
GRADE I	25%	25%	40%	65%
GRADE II*	25%	20%	40%	65%
GRADE II	25%	$12\frac{1}{2}$% #	—	40%
KEY BUILDINGS IN CONSERVATION AREAS	20%	ON MERIT	—	30%
OTHER GOOD BUILDINGS IN CONSERVATION AREAS	15%	ON MERIT	—	30%
OTHER HISTORIC BUILDINGS	15%	ON MERIT	—	30%

† The County Council do not normally grant aid buildings in the City Conservation Area or works which are being grant aided by the HBMC.
# The County Council do not normally grant aid Grade II buildings outside conservation areas.

and Monuments Commission, the County Council may make grants to certain buildings in the rural area (see Table Nine).

WORKS ELIGIBLE FOR GRANT AID

In order to qualify for historic building grant, works must involve *repairs* which help to retain the *existing structural or architectural integrity* of the building. Thus works such as new partitions, staircases, windows and other alterations which are intended to improve existing accommodation will not be eligible; nor will repairs which involve parts of a building which are relatively modern additions or alterations with no architectural or historic merit.

Although grant aid for maintenance is included within the scope of the 1962 Act, this is not allowed in practice and repairs have to be of a substantial nature before a grant application is considered.

The only exception to the fundamental rule which limits grant aid to works of repair are Section 10 grants, which can be given for works of repair *or enhancement*. Enhancement may include demolition, reinstatement of missing features, work to bring part of a building into use or the carrying out of feasibility studies.

The following schedule gives guidance on the works and services which normally qualify for repair grants, and those which do not.

Works and services normally qualifying for repair grant
Underpinning of foundations.
Repair and rebuilding of internal and external walls.
Repair and replacement of floor and roof timbers.
Repair and replacement of rainwater goods.
Reslating or retiling of roofs.
Repair and rebuilding of chimney stacks.
Treatment of timber against insect and fungal attack.
Repointing of brick and stonework.
Repair and replacement of doors and windows.
Repair of internal features (cornices, panelling, etc).
Redecoration following the above repairs.

Professional fees on grant eligible work charged by Architects, Quantity Surveyors and Structural Engineers.
Value Added Tax on grant eligible work if the applicant cannot reclaim the tax.

Works not eligible for grant aid
Minor repairs, such as replacement of odd slates, reglazing, painting and clearing out of gutters.
Installation of a damp proof course.
Works of alteration and improvement.
Renewal or repair of services such as electrical, gas, water, plumbing and drainage systems. (Exceptions can be made for the cost of disturbance to such services as an essential part of carrying out other repairs to the fabric of the building).
Works which are the subject of insurance claims.
Works which have received house improvement grant.
Works involving structural *upgrading* to accommodate new uses.

GRANT CEILINGS

Some authorities impose minimum and/or maximum limits on the size of individual grants in order to maintain efficiency, and to spread funds as widely as possible. If a minimum limit is set, there is a danger that important repairs which are limited in cost, such as dry rot eradication, may fall outside the scope of grant aid. The implication of this is serious in those cases where owners cannot afford to carry out repairs without financial support. For this reason, the City Council does not at present impose lower limits on grant contributions.

Similarly a number of repair schemes are very expensive and are only viable if large grants are available. Imposition of arbitrary upper limits would mean that repairs may not be implemented and buildings placed at risk.

REBUILDING OF FACADES

A basic principle inherent in the philosophy of the conservation of old buildings is that, if a structure has reached such a state where continued use is impossible and necessary repairs are totally uneconomic, then the wisest course of action is demolition and redevelopment. This approach avoids the dubious practice of 'preservation at all costs', and allows gradual and piecemeal renewal of our towns and cities to take place. Because of a lack of faith in modern architecture, a preference for traditional building styles or the contribution of a particular facade in a street scene, there has been a recent tendency to encourage the reconstruction of unrepairable or derelict buildings 'in facsimile'. This process is not repair; and therefore conservation grants are not normally offered in these cases.

MEANS TEST

The Historic Buildings and Monuments Commission do not offer grants to multi-national companies, or other large institutions and bodies with considerable assets, on the basis that this would be an improper use of public funds. On schemes operated jointly the City Council is expected to advise the Commission if it is believed that an applicant falls into the above categories. The applicant is then asked to provide financial information indicating profit levels and assets. The success of this monitoring process is obviously unpredictable and depends to a great extent on the intuition of conservation staff.

The City Council do not operate such a means test, but for all projects with eligible repair costs of over £100,000 the specific financial circumstances of the scheme are considered. The grant is then set at a level which makes the project viable in terms of normal development practice.

NEW PURCHASERS

The Historic Buildings and Monuments Commission do not normally offer grants for buildings which have been purchased within the past four years, because it is considered that the purchase price should have reflected the need for any repairs. The City Council recognises that many factors influence property prices and that even where the purchase price of a building does reflect its condi-

tion, this will not automatically lead to the repairs being implemented. Nevertheless, the Council looks carefully at all grant applications from new purchasers and may require additional information before the application can be considered.

The Council does not normally offer grants for properties which have been recently purchased for the purpose of subdivision or major alteration and improvement. An exception to this policy may be made if the purchase has been made for the express purpose of restoring the building (eg by a preservation trust) or if the building is in an advanced state of dereliction and the new purchase is the last chance to save it. An exception may also be made if the work is to be undertaken by a non-profit making organisation (eg a housing association).

PHASED REPAIRS

The City Council recognises that many owners cannot afford to carry out comprehensive repairs as a single scheme, and is normally willing to arrange for grants to be made available for a phased programme of repairs, possibly extending over a number of years. However, this has to be on the understanding that grants for later phases will be dependent upon the resources available to the Council at the time of application.

GRANT CONDITIONS

A number of conditions are attached to an offer of grant with the aims of controlling quality of workmanship, additional works, date of completion, resale of the property, etc:

Additional works

Because of the unpredictable nature of repair works to historic buildings, it is common to discover during the course of a contract, that additional works are needed to remedy defects which could not have been foreseen at the preparation stages. In these circumstances, it is usual to recommend further grant towards the extra costs involved. However, advantage is often taken of this flexibility by agents who have taken insufficient care in the preparation of repair schedules, and then expect an automatic increase in grant to cover their lack of thoroughness. Additional grants are only considered for work that could not have been reasonably foreseen at the planning stages.

Applications for extra grant towards increased costs due to other circumstances, such as inflation, or an unforeseen rise in the price of materials, are considered on merit.

Quality of work

In cases where the quality of repair works does not meet the standards set by the City Council and Historic Buildings and Monuments Commission, and it is impracticable for such defective work to be remedied, some or all of the approved grant may be withheld.

Grant Recovery

Grant giving authorities normally stipulate that in the event of a property being sold within a certain period of payment of the grant being made, then some or all of the grant may be recovered, according to circumstances. All property sales within the District are monitored on a weekly basis by conservation staff, with this condition in mind.

There is a presumption that a grant will automatically be recovered if property is resold within three years of the final grant payment, unless the applicant can demonstrate to the satisfaction of the Council that a nett financial loss has been incurred in the process, or that there are other exceptional circumstances involved.

Additional Works as a Condition of Grant

On occasions it may be appropriate to stipulate, as a condition of receiving grant, that certain additional works should be carried out by the applicant, that will not attract grant aid in themselves. For example, as a condition of giving grant for roof repairs it may be stipulated that the rainwater goods be repainted. In this way minor but significant repairs and improvements to historic buildings can be achieved by persuasion, and at no cost to the City Council.

Quinquennial Surveys

Since the conservation programme began, there have been a few cases of buildings which have received grant aid subsequently falling into disrepair through lack of subsequent care and maintenance. In order to avoid this problem, where the City Council makes a grant contribution of £10,000 or more towards the cost of a repair scheme, the owner will be obliged to submit to the Council at five yearly intervals, at his own expense, a survey by a suitably qualified person which describes the condition of the building in question.

Acknowledgement of Grant Aid

It is not uncommon for press coverage describing major repair and refurbishment schemes to make no reference to the significant financial contribution which has been made by public authorities. Public awareness of the important role of the City Council and the Historic Buildings and Monuments Commission is therefore diminished.

Where the City Council makes a significant financial contribution towards the cost of a repair or refurbishment project, the applicant and his agents should acknowledge the grant aid in any press coverage, and on any site board.

INDEX